no_memory

by Stanley Lieber

Written 2018 – 2022

This book was typeset (`troff -ms|lp -dstdout|ps2pdf`) in URW Garamond No. 8 by the author, using a MNT Reform laptop running the 9front operating system.

MASSIVE FICTIONS
massivefictions.com

ISBN-13: 978-1-6781-7716-4

no_memory

the_town

Every moment of his youth apart from its dream was forgotten
— Bertolt Brecht, *Baal*

▦ West Berlin, Indiana. 2049.

It was time to dry out. Like so many of his contemporaries he'd made his way to West Berlin, to take in the waters, to expose himself recklessly to the moribund, exquisite desolation, to luxuriate in the low bandwidth and the utter lack of interest in—or from—the outside world.

Newcomers recognized each other easily by the pale strip of flesh bracketing their eyes, where their visors had been semi-permanently attached, never before removed. The visors would be useless here. They wouldn't even work as sunglasses.

He scanned the imposing blue ridgeline but found no antennas. The town was situated in the cleft of an extinct river valley. It was easy to forget sometimes that anything lay beyond, if, in fact, anything did. Mold was everywhere.

Everything felt familiar.

SL had never even seen the place before moving in. Not with his own eyes, anyway, and his pale strip of flesh was by now starting to fade in reverse, colored over by IRL.

He stopped the record player and returned his original Fontana pressing of Scott Walker's *Tilt* to its pristine sleeve. Filed it on the shelf. He liked the record, but tonight the input was overwhelming him.

He needed silence.

He'd come to West Berlin with a friend. Perhaps *friend* was too strong a term. A contact. They shared an affinity for a particular misconception of West Berlin culture. Old books, music. Of course, that forgotten world was by now long gone, if it had ever truly existed. Now that he actually lived here he tended to doubt it, but that was beside the point. They shared a consensual interest in the material. One could say they were willfully credulous.

Yes.

SL sipped his tea.

"What's your name, anyway?" his friend finally asked. "I mean, your real name. In real life."

It was a dubious proposition. Did SL *sound* like an alias?

"Ray," SL lied. "Call me Ray."

"Okay," his friend said easily, satisfied for now to spackle on yet more bullshit. They'd reconcile the details later.

They rode the lateral elevator crosswise down to breakfast in the hotel restaurant. SL ordered his usual scrambled eggs with toast, and in its place he received a small plate heaping with pungent, salted bacon.

"You planning to eat that?" his friend asked.

The poor fool was oblivious to the spiritual consequences of consuming swine flesh. SL nudged his plate across the table, careful to avoid spilling his tea. He'd spare his friend the prepared lecture.

The morning sun ducked behind a crowding murder of clouds and the pair soon followed suit, finishing off the remainder of their meal in silence before making their excuses and retiring to the sheltering darkness of their separate rooms.

Hotel surveillance promptly detected network traffic passing between the rooms, a blatant violation of the ToS.

The response was automated and immediate, brooking no appeals to *Be reasonable, man,* or *Hey, I paid for this room,* or *Just a few minutes more.*

dropped connection

▦ SL, beleaguered protagonist:

"Every novel is somebody's first," he announced, by way of introducing the impending storyline.

SL's friend, long-suffering sidekick:

"Sometimes, I think I don't know who I am anymore." He sighed, happily, and downed his coffee.

Preamble concluded, the main cast could now see their way to getting on with the tale.

The hotel was a couple of centuries old, give or take a few decades. Not that the *casual* visitor could tell, what with all the layers of hi-res renovations. It followed then that the parts which appeared to be the oldest were in fact the most recently revitalized. The hotel restaurant, for example, had been rebooted just last month. Its bar, a recent addition, was now canon.

SL liked the hotel restaurant. He'd pack up his supplies and sit down there in a booth for half the day, reading his comics and sketching portraits the other guests. Most of them would calm down if he agreed to show them his work.

SL's friend didn't like to be sketched. When SL picked up his pencil his friend would just up and leave the room, often without saying a word. Suited SL fine. As time wore on he began to regret having invited the imbecile in the first place. Why had he agreed to come, anyway? And why had SL agreed to take a pass over the imbecile's recovery exegesis? Just who was the bigger idiot, here?

No bacon this morning. It had only taken them a month to figure out he wasn't going to eat it.

The fines for attempted network connections were piling up. Fortunately, SL was fucking rich.

He'd sit there in the restaurant and wait for something remarkable to happen. Something remarkable rarely did, and so he remarked only rarely. During the interminable delay between minor piques of interest SL would jot down whatever observations occurred to him, recording it all faithfully in his recovery journal. Just the facts, just as recovery theory demanded. Scrawling out page after page in minute detail, mundane mechanized responses to the predictable plot machinations he witnessed all around him. He supposed that this was what they wanted. He described in some detail what it must have been like for them to probe the shared hallucination for the familiar topography of his face. Let them sort that one out.

Nowadays, *he* could look in the mirror.

Or, in this case, a salt shaker. His reflection bent and wobbled as the unsteady shaker tipped itself completely over, a server having bumped into SL's table on her way through the dining room to extinguish a small fire in the no smoking section.

SL dropped his pen.

The quiet here was near total. Unbelievable. SL found it was conducive to memory, which was something of a mixed blessing given his many uncomfortable reasons for having retreated to West Berlin.

West Berlin... has   many roles.
— John F. Kennedy, 25 July 1961

On the one hand he could barely keep in mind why he was here. On the other hand he really didn't want to be here in the first place.

And now he was out of hands.

Most of his personal equipment had been confiscated upon arrival, but SL still concealed within his shirtsleeve a backup pair of data gloves, folded neatly into a palm–sized green square, pressed into the equally diminutive Faraday pouch laid smooth against his bare arm. He could feel it there, cool against his skin.

Hastily, he ripped open the pouch and slipped on the data gloves.

What do you mean?

He knew what he was doing.

▦ SL's friend insisted upon following him around with a camera. Offline, so, technically still permissible under the hotel's ToS. Didn't stop SL from getting annoyed.

"Quit pointing that thing at me," SL would say, and his friend would quit, for a while, and sometimes for the rest of the day. But the camera somehow always reappeared.

SL had gotten enough of this treatment back at home.

Breakfast now consisted of reading the paper—a traditional, paper newspaper—alone. Half the paper's weight comprised loose leaf advertisements printed on a slick paper that stuck to his fingers whenever he tried to remove them. Coupons for stores and restaurants that did not have operating locations in this tiny resort town.

It was a local paper.

The supposed news itself was all *too* relevant—hyper specific POV reporting that assumed an intricate knowledge of local personages and customs. SL possessed neither. He pored over the paper anyway, enjoying the certain... *je ne sais quois...* of this textual delivery system for what to him amounted to null verbiage. Glancing at his wristwatch he confirmed that doing so still passed the time.

In the afternoons he could most often be found by the pool. This unlikely juxtaposition of venue and artist inspired in him the farsical delusion that he could somehow defend his sketchbooks from the malevolent perturbations of screaming, splashing children. Found that he couldn't. So, why then was he sitting by the pool? He wanted to hand the children back their visors.

Pouting was unlike himself, but there it was.

He was settling into a routine, and yes, he was still cheating.

SL's friend had found other things to do with his time. He no longer presented as online. Zero contact for the last month. For his part, SL had idly contrived any number of schemes for flagging his friend's attention, but finally admitted to himself that it might be better to simply let the friendship drop.

He wondered now how his friend would react when he found out no one was paying his hotel bill.

SL wanted to think this could work. So far, being dropped into an environment of strict network unavailability had cut his online time in half (Alas, WiFi finds a way). Without the visor, and without authorized access to the local mesh, friction was sufficient that he needed to discriminate carefully between potential activities. He planned in advance, then scrambled to complete the items on his checklist before his connection fizzled out.

And, no logging. With bandwidth constrained, something had to give.

Often, even remembering what he'd just done proved to be a challenge.

⊞ It would require a non-trivial measure of an as yet unspecified effort to deduce just when SL had arrived at the hotel. He no longer pretended to have any earthly idea. It had to have been before Christmas (he remembered attending a Christmas party in the hotel lobby), but before that, who could say?

His friend might remember.

But, no.

He knew why he was here, in West Berlin, and that was to forget about such things. People, situations just such as these. Taking a cue from his absent friend, he, too, would find something else to do with his time.

Today he ordered lunch in his room and settled in to commit more atrocities of language to his recovery journal. The exegesis continued.

In the long afternoons he would sometimes walk into town and gaze at the meandering traffic as it trundled along the main road, or purchase frivolous items at the drug store. Today he needed blank cassettes and chewing gum. And they were all out of gum.

On his way to the checkout SL ignored the spinner rack of comic books that had suddenly and conspicuously interpolated itself between his handbasket and the register.

Nobody asked to see his ID.

Walking around town would have been pleasant if not for the intrusive presence of overzealous NPCs, bent on chucking beer cans at his head, at suspiciously equally spaced intervals. Too bad for them, he saw through the thin veneer of their shitty programming to the underlying algorithm.

SL varied his own route to compensate. He found that the algorithm *he* chose was effective for only a few iterations, so eventually he had to alternate algorithms via an additional, algorithmically generated algorithm.

All of this was possible only because he had held on to the data gloves.

When finally he was caught in the act, he had had to plead with the hotel administration not to kick him out of his room. At length the stern panel of twenty-somethings had relented, but required that he hand over the contraband data gloves, temporary visor, and related accessories. SL went along with it, for now. What else was he going to do? Leave?

▦ Friends had been trying to convince him for years that he should come to West Berlin. "It would be good for your art," they always said, vaguely intimating... what, exactly? Well, now that he was here, there was nothing to do. There was no *scene.* He supposed they'd gotten rid of him, after all.

SL was up early to perform his stretches. And once again he had thrown out his back. Thus disenlivened, he sat back down with his tea and newspaper. As usual, nothing was happening. What had he expected?

Most of the bars and strip clubs were closed this early in the morning. Even the drug store and the VFW. Sometimes, an Internet would be working down at the VFW during the day, and they would take pity on him, and they would let him in, and he would sit there all day, drawing. No such luck today.

For a city of three million (SL could scarcely believe that such a small place could still exist) the streets were invariably clogged during the day. Where were these people *going* during business hours? Also, the town's homeless were invisible—or at least, he almost never saw any. Maybe here in West Berlin the powers that be had actually executed their war on poverty. Or maybe they simply executed their poor.

No, there was no scene to speak of. As a consequence SL was left to invent his own trouble.

He'd work something out.

From one end of the city to the other was a journey of about eight miles. SL traversed the full length every day, before lunch, after lunch, striving to soak up anything that might enrich the balance of his recovery journal. Whatever it was his friends had been so insistent he needed to absorb, he was certainly soaking in it, but nothing was seeping in, and he still wasn't finding its level. His calves always ached but his health never seemed to improve. He was tired of trying so hard only to have nothing to show for his efforts.

He wasn't drawing.

At least he'd stopped bringing the data gloves. Along with his wallet, keys, ID, pocket knife, and water, he'd also chosen to leave behind the contraband gear. It was all too bulky, too heavy, too easily stuck to the sweat of his skin in the heat. And he never knew when he was going to have to try and outrun a giant pickup truck.

SL hadn't figured on spending so much time here, alone, in this ridiculous little town.

He drained the remainder of his tea onto the sidewalk and returned the plastic cup and saucer to the sidewalk dispenser.

The incessant buzzing of cicadas left him in a strange mood.

▦ "Do you put on your data gloves *before* or *after* you pee in the morning?"

There was a reason SL never attended these meetings. Hadn't, since he'd arrived. He'd been warned in advance.

"Both," he interjected, annoyed. Of course he took them off to piss. Unlike these cretins, he guessed.

He stood up to leave.

No paper today. Something he'd vaguely overheard about a general strike. Apparently only observed by the press.

Otherwise, today was exactly the same as every other day. Tea, eggs, stretch, walk, watch, walk, stretch, sit. A rhythm scarcely broken by the absence of printed nothingness. Maybe he should be saving his money.

There were always welcoming faces down at the VFW. He shot some pool, asked the old men questions about California. They were generous with their stories. One of them had been to the Mission District before the city had gotten rid of the titty bars (his words). A place with comic books varnished to the men's room walls.

None of them used anymore.

SL had never served and so he didn't have much to contribute in return. He'd mention his father and they'd nod. It was usually good for a couple of drinks.

By Christmas time, this place would be full of kids trying to climb onto Santa's lap, but today it was just a bunch of sad, old men avoiding eye contact, trying not to mention the Internet.

What had really happened, back in 1993? He knew of course that by early October the war had silently kicked off, but the papers back then—and TV, and religion—had all failed to recognize what it would inevitably add up to, once the dispossessed had finally been disposed of. The familiar cycle: changes that were at first gradual, but accelerated smoothly along a menacing, nearly vertical curve until, even before the reboot, continuity was arcing, spiraling, babbling out of control. No longer was this to be the staid, predictable march from trope to cliché to signature recurring trademark. Trademark! And now trademarked again, for this derivation was assuredly all new, all different, a departure from, but shining example of, the once and future downwardly spiraling status quo. Here was the final dissolution of reading comprehension. *E pluribus nullus, ad infinitum.*

For SL's part, he was glad that the papers were back in print. It gave him something to do with his hands.

VETERANS OF FOREIGN WIDE AREA NETWORKS

SL stared at the tarnished bronze plaque while the others took their shots. He missed whatever remarks the men made while he was standing there, slack-jawed, gaping at their knickknacks. Someone had just mentioned "Bay Area rents," and the place fell silent as a pre-war visor.

SL edged his way out of the room and made for the front door.

This wasn't his fight.

Back at the hotel, SL fidgeted nervously, unsure if he should break into his emergency supply of disposables. He'd been doing so well these past few weeks. Not even checking his stocks. And now here he was contemplating an entire evening spent drowning his many sorrows in everything he'd been denying himself for a month. Like nothing at all had changed.

Well, maybe *nothing* *at all had changed.*

▓▓ Contradictions of life in the hotel: The restaurant was situated on a separate floor from its restrooms. SL took the stairs, mainly because the lateral elevator was still only moving sideways. Worse, upon exiting one was obliged to pass through a hall of archival material commemorating the hotel's past advertising campaigns. Egressing the nostalgia tour, guests were scanned and registered as willing participants in whatever current campaign was in the offing, details TBA. A mandatory, implicit endorsement of precisely the horseshit people came here to escape. SL was glad to bypass it.

Walking back upstairs presented its own challenges: namely, interception by the hotel's dedicated brand coaching staff. No matter how many times SL refused their services, the pitch remained the same: *Come with us if you want to live.* SL invariably declined, citing his self-evident lack of willpower (*e.g.*, rehab).

And they hadn't killed him yet.

For some reason, all the motor vehicles in town had begun presenting as if they rolled on green wheels. Somehow, SL had failed to notice this before. He figured there must be some significance, perhaps an exculpatory one, but he couldn't quite put his finger on it. Green rubber? Was it *political?* Guys down at the VFW just stared at him whenever he brought it up. So he let the matter drop, and soon he forgot all about it, as if all wheels everywhere had always been green. A lot of things around here seemed to work that way. Just let it go, and maybe soon you'll forget all about it. The practical applications...

SL patted the hidden compartment in his trousers. The envelope was still there.

And what had become of his friend during all these weeks?

"Long time no snark," SL's friend beamed, genuinely happy to see him.

"Yeah," SL allowed, sounding almost as deflated as he felt.

Thank Christ for room tone. Whatever his friend had said in reply was lost in a burst of static as his gear adjusted to the room's new normal. SL now paused to calibrate his haptics manually. In the weeks since he'd logged in there had been some considerable drift in his settings. He ignored the inconvenience and tried to look natural.

Afterwards, SL was disappointed in himself. Again, he'd broken a winning streak only to come away feeling worse than when he'd logged in. Worst of all, the ground was shifting beneath him. Even as he stood still, his remaining equipment was obsoleting, would soon no longer be *able* to login.

And then where would he be?

⠿ The lateral elevator was still stuck on sideways, so SL climbed the stairs to his room. The coaching staff was strangely AWOL this evening, a welcome absence in the hallway's otherwise pristine blandness.

Room cleaners had moved all his books. And, it seemed, removed all his bookmarks as well. He supposed as a sort of commentary upon the general state of his room. Fair enough.

SL colonized the balcony with a minimum of fuss. Just him and his cup of tea, not even the folded daily newspaper. The indigenous population of his table had scattered upon first sight of his tattered boxer shorts, surrendering whatever claim they might have otherwise proffered in the absence of universally recognized property rights.

SL sat down in his chair, feeling anything but the conquering hero, his destiny anything but manifest.

The town had changed since he'd arrived. Nothing he'd actually observed, mind, but it stood to reason things would change, didn't it? Even if only by virtue of his sudden appearance in the narrative. Anyway, whatever.

Dull care washed over him, subsiding with the smog as the morning sun burned away all remaining conscious thought.

From then to now he hadn't allowed himself to approach the memory of what had come before. Masking such awareness with the background clatter (such as it was) of the hustle and bustle here in town. The ticker tape advanced at intervals, faintly audible in the cradling semi-silence.

The sound was annoying.

Who, then, had he been? No one here seemed to recognize him, so he could rule out intersectional notoriety. There were no clues as to his interests amongst the few personal belongings he kept in his room, unless of course you counted the books, which he had never attempted to do. His personal library was distinguished primarily by its failure to establish a clear theme—this scattershot syncretism seemed to be all that remained of whomever he might have been before he arrived here. In any case, he had forgotten the question. He repeated the inventory of his room, twice, each time promptly arriving at this same dead-end of forgetfulness, and then decided it was time for lunch.

There isn't much, in all honesty, that can't be conveyed through simple language. This was a cornerstone of recovery theory, even though most patients immediately recognized it as bullshit. There was *nothing* that could be conveyed through simple language, nothing that could be conveyed, *at all.* Each advancing column of society asserted anew this naked poverty of comprehension through the mechanically ratcheting acceleration of immediate—literally, cybernetic—feedback.

Just because it couldn't be expressed in words didn't mean it wasn't true.

SL rubbed his eyes.

Sans visor.

⊞ Finally and at long last knowing himself, SL wandered into the countryside. He'd sneak out of the hotel before dawn, while the brand coaches were still asleep, and break for the woods. In these parts there were no isolated stands of trees. Every branch of the forest connected somehow back to its trunk. You followed the leaves to the sky, then followed the veins back down to the ground. You never escaped the tree.

Within this semantic forest one typically encountered more trash than on the street. A catalog of discarded items, some of them immediately saleable, some useful personally. Today SL encountered both varieties of green trash, and immediately he made plans for its collection and dispersal.

The creeks were similarly full of litter. Sometimes SL came upon piles of unopened MREs. He knew which shops back in town would be interested in the expired meals. Caches of crap turned back into cash.

SL would perch himself on an outcropping alongside the creek and feel the cool water soaking into his shoes. Mosquitoes skipped across the reflecting surface, dodging expertly as he tried to swat them away. Mold, everywhere.

He had no memory of why he'd come here.

Twenty minutes deeper into the woods (though somehow still within earshot of rush hour traffic), the trail opened up onto the abandoned ruins of what once must have been a house. Like everything else in the town, it felt familiar.

On days when it rained the whole town stank of cat piss. In reality it had to have been something else because SL had never seen a cat in West Berlin. Or maybe it was just that they'd all been hiding from him. Whatever the cause, the air, and everything else, was stifling.

SL couldn't get back to his room quickly enough. He propelled himself into the shower.

Breakfast was a cul-de-sac. He steered himself to his table, turned himself around, and steered himself right back out again. Another routine sublimated within the blank, gray miscategorization of his user icon. This, too, flew in the face of recovery theory. The automatic mechanisms he had hoped to finally transcend had been replaced with labor intensive equivalents—though these, too, were beyond his willingness to comprehend consciously. They had him working against himself. Life imitating farce, world without end.

It had all gone quiet enough that he was once again prepared to wonder about the fate of his friend, whose name he could no longer remember.

That would complicate a search.

▦ The buildings were all connected. (All of them?)
Yes, underground, just like the trees of the semantic forest.
For SL it had seemed like just another rumor, probably bull-
shit, but he intended to find out for sure.

The foundations of the old school building still occupied the equivalent of a city block, up on a hill overlooking
the town. Here SL located a service tunnel that supposedly
joined the school to the covert subterranean network.

Interference was light, so SL was able to confirm that
the school's buried roots stretched at least to the abandoned
motel-cum-apartment building down the street before he
decided it was time for lunch. He unfolded a sandwich and
apple slices from his backpack and unscrewed his jumbo ther-
mos of tea, admiring the decrepit splendor of the vast ball-
room into which his tunnel had suddenly opened. This
place, too, was falling apart. He surmised that no one had
been down here in quite some time. Even the trash was
obsolete.

Same routine, different day. SL was scarfing down his
lunch in the basement of yet another abandoned building,
this one also tethered to the secret network of tunnels,

though at the moment he wasn't sure exactly which building he'd stumbled into. Ambient lighting was nil. He ate in total darkness.

He could still hear the traffic.

After a few months of this he'd managed to map out an intimidating web of tunnels. Carefully, he marked them all down on a big piece of graph paper that he folded into triangles and stuffed into his backpack. Sometimes when he pulled out the map it would snag on a pair of his contraband data gloves, flipping them carelessly onto the floor. He'd snatch them back up, guiltily, but there was no signal down here in the tunnels, and anyway he hadn't even been trying to use them, so at length he'd just shrug and stow them away again. It *did* make him feel more secure, just knowing they were in there.

I'm sorry, *why* was he doing this?

By now his map was crisscrossed with densely annotated routes to and from various branching arteries beneath the town. Useless, since he had no intention of ever visiting them again. He had no one to share the map with, nor any desire to do so, which, he suddenly realized, he regarded as a species of progress.

He folded up the map and stuck it into a crack in one of the tunnel walls.

Back to the previous routine, then. Holding court on his balcony (although there were no well-wishers, relatives, or advertisers vying for his attention) from the petty optimism of breakfast to the depressing dregs of lunch. SL ate his eggs. There was nothing else to do but think. There was nothing else he *wanted* to do but think. Was this, too, then, a sign of progress? The flame of his addiction, the perpetual interplay of point and counterpoint at long last extinguished?

It seemed unlikely.

All the same, SL observed, given his newfound equanimity, it might finally be time to go home.

the_city

Note: You can't find this shit in a handbook.
— Ice Cube, *How To Survive In South Central*

▦ Megatokyo, Indiana. 2049.

SL was back at work. Tough interrogation, re: his furlough in West Berlin. Well, it sure as shit wasn't *this* place, if you know what I mean. They said they knew what he meant. He was already sorry he'd come back, but at least the bandwidth here was civilized.

Most of the work he'd left behind on his desk was still there, but now it was buried beneath more of the same, sad stuff. Striated sediment accumulated through the usual organic processes during his pre-approved absence. SL swept it all away with a single gesture, slashing at the horizon with his shimmering, black-gloved hand. Better by half to start from inbox zero.

"Have a good summer?" SL's friend looked refreshed. First he'd heard from him since the kiss-off in West Berlin. How long had it been, anyway?

"Shut the fuck up," SL said, and emptied his styrofoam cup of coffee onto his friend's new shoes. Nike AJV, cult classics. So-called "Moon Boots."

Obviously counterfeit.

Multicolored tendrils snaking, now vibrating, now suddenly tilting ninety degrees to flash on a cross–sectional view of flat square sprites, arranged in an orderly patchwork of checked, fluorescent light. SL could tell because he could see some of the pixels. He moved them around with his eyes, dumbly relying on his gloves for a secondary axis. Whatever you called it.

Drilling down, he paused intermittently to evaluate a list of bullet points, loosely guided by company policy as haptic feedback intermittently failed. Some of the material he would ingest consciously, but the bulk of it was archived for later, offline perusal. Of course, he'd never get around to it.

At last he shuttered his visor and switched back to audio, bounding through the remainder at 2.5x suggested playback speed. Continuously distracted by unrelated matters, he had had to start over four times, losing his stream of consciousness at different points each time. The interruptions impacted his retention, which called into the question the whole enterprise.

The backlog was brutal. Even before he completed the mandatory six months re-training, he'd still be expected to pick up some of the leads his people had let drop. High risk credit ratings desperate to... whatever it was they were desperate to do. The relevant factor was that in their desperation they were more likely to fall for his company's pitch—a high interest, unsecured line of credit that stood up pre-charged nearly to its limit. Exceeding the cap incurred exorbitant fees, which was where the company realized its profits. Something like seventy-eight percent of new customers immediately charged their account to just below its upper limit, which, since they had reliably failed to read the fine print, *actually* pushed them well into the red. Transactions were never denied, and thus the fees began to accrue even before the virtual ink on their virtual credit agreements had virtually dried.

SL didn't care much about the minutiae. His actual job was managing comfort counselors, who in turn serviced loan technicians, who finally interfaced directly with customers. Most of his time was spent manually transcribing their efficiency reports into spreadsheets that he later e-mailed to his own boss. Or, increasingly, firing the loan techs for not having made their numbers that week.

Fully immersed in his computing environment, his arms were flailing around like there was something wrong with him.

Nobody approached his desk.

The stairwells were left unguarded. As far as SL could tell there was virtually no security, no countermeasures had been deployed to prevent unauthorized staff from moving freely between floors. But this couldn't have been the company's intention, so walking up and down the stairs simply wasn't done. Tacitly compliant, managers never even attempted it.

Still, Nistopher, one of SL's peers in management, was curious. One afternoon he waited until the corridor was empty, then casually Nis-walked up to the second level. *You'll never believe what happened next.* It surprised him, too: a corridor identical to the one he'd left behind on the first floor. "As above, so below," Nistopher confirmed, and then silently returned to his desk, reassured by this valuable confirmation of the universe's fearful symmetry.

Unbeknownst to Nistopher, the moment he'd entered the stairwell his employment had been terminated. However, owing to a glitch in [redacted], he was not informed of the fact until fully three weeks had elapsed. No, he was not to be compensated for the shifts he had worked during the interim, either, although the company did continue to let him into the building, and he continued to do his job.

Nistopher didn't seem to mind. Once they finally got around to telling him he'd been fired, he simply stood up, left his desk and personal effects as they were, and walked silently out of the building.

Just like the Rapture, a near-peer cracked, unhelpfully.

SL counted the days until his next vacation. As a manager his time off was subject to the needs of the business. He didn't have a contract (management were employed "at will"), so all he could do was submit his request and hope that it didn't get overtaken by events in the field. This was the price of sitting in the big chair with the *shiatsu* massage.

But there was always a bigger chair. SL's own boss, when she was not on vacation, wielded her limited influence with a wild and unpredictable caprice, carpet bombing from high altitude. He tried to stay off her radar, even though he was still obliged to touch base, insert his deep input, massage the numbers *(shiatsu* or no), and reconcile his own receipts at simultaneous, pre-programmed intervals. He had then only to sit back and wait for her response, which, while unpredictable, was inevitably bombastic. One might say, in an utterly predictable way.

He'd better take this train of thought offline.

Megatokyo nodes were popping up all over. Zoo York, ATL, Emerald City, Texas, Michigan, and Oklahoma. "Hell," SL thought, "If it can happen here, it can happen anywhere."

Unigov, the colloquial name adopted by the city of Megatokyo *(né* Indianapolis) to describe its ever-expanding consolidation of node cities worldwide, was finally beginning to function as intended. Better access to EMS shipping leveraged lower prices for everyone. Free press, free movement, total surveillance of same.

Besides, municipal autonomy had long ago been proven not to work.

In spite of all this, West Berlin and other points south had, so far, avoided being swallowed up into the burgeoning Yellow Belt. This circumstance afforded certain opportunities for trade. Margins could be skillfully skated to slice out a meager profit, for those unfortunate enough to be frozen out of the Unigov's legitimate economic activity.

SL had opinions about the arrangement.

▦ "If everybody's from Megatokyo then nobody's from Megatokyo."

Nistopher was at it again. He'd come over to SL's personal pan apt after his last day at work, and now, beer in hand, he held forth on matters personal and political.

"Citizenship's not a zero sum game," SL offered, evenly. "The whole world could join Megatokyo, who cares?"

"Everybody who lives somewhere else," Nistopher countered adamantly, and sipped his beer. He poured some of it out on his hand, made a fist. Slammed it down on the kitchen counter. "I used to live somewhere else."

"Well, now that you're no longer chained to the company maybe you can think about living somewhere else, again."

"In this economy?" was all Nistopher could muster. He stared out the kitchen window, straining through the greasy fingerprints on his visor. His eyes crossed.

SL stole a glance at the wall clock.

"Say, why don't we move this into the living room. Maybe we can pick up a signal from the office before they start shutting down for the day. I've got something I want to show you."

"Don't let me catch you off the Internet again."
Nistopher was imitating the raspy, cigarette ravaged voice SL
affected (SL had never smoked) with his subordinates at
work. He staggered and nearly toppled SL's rickety old CRT
display. Haha, he was drunk.

"Okay, good one, buddy," SL said, patting his longtime
cubemate on the shoulder. There had to be some way to get
him out of here before he puked on the carpet. In addition,
SL still had to be at work in the morning, earliest. What to
do?

"I tell you," Nistopher told him, "I don't know if I'll
ever be coming back." He was bargaining now with chips
he'd already frittered away. "And *that woman* can kiss my
underweight ass." Here Nistopher referred to their mutual
supervisor, whom SL had also found it hard to work with.
Nis seemed at last to be wrapping up the series finale of his
long-running soliloquy, piloted and premiered so many
years ago. SL nodded one last time and patted his
ex-coworker's arm a bit more firmly, locking the door as
Nistopher finally exited the apt. Roll credits.

That could have gone better, SL thought, with some
regret, but at least now it was over.

SL tapped his visor and shut himself down for the night.

Fell asleep thinking about the Internet.

Simpler times.

Promotion. The company had graciously moved SL up
to the second floor. It was very much like the first floor, but
this time with windows. From his desk SL could *just* make
out his car in the open-air parking lot. (There weren't many
open-air parking lots left in this part of the world.)

Work was okay. He now spent the bulk of his days
mentoring a fellow who had moved into his old position,
down on the first floor. His one and only direct report. Not
a recipe for swift advancement, but then he'd been promised
more direct reports in the next quarter.

On the day of THE BIG FIRE, SL tried to make sure his man made it out of the building alive. That was what you did and that was who you did it for: the man beside (or in this case, directly beneath) you. Managers on the second floor were able to break their windows and leap out onto the street, some suffering broken ankles, but all surviving the calamity. Most everyone on the first floor was trapped, locked in by the failing security system. Those few who had dared to venture up the stairwell would later find out that their employment had been retroactively terminated, (à la SL's old pal Nistopher). Owing to their brazen abrogation of company policy, insurance would refuse to cover their injuries.

SL's man did not survive. He'd seen a handful of his coworkers running up the stairs, and then, falling back on his training, decided for himself not to deviate from company policy. SL had already determined to let him pass, but, owing to his sudden flare-up of integrity, his man never appeared.

SL's hands had been tied. There was nothing he could have done.

A year or so later, promoted again. SL now had his own button on the lateral elevator, which transported him directly to his desk. (Okay, all right, everybody used the same "smart" button, but when SL pushed it he was delivered to his own desk. Progress?) It was a perquisite unique to his new status as a third level.

The new building was further downtown, in the heart of the city, and was very much taller than the firebombed wreckage of his old office back in the two-story walk-up. This place had history, gravitas, *balls.* A hundred years ago it had been hoisted into the air, twisted on its base, and then drilled back down into the earth nearly a block down the street. And that was only foreplay, foreshadowing renovations that would ultimately climax in its certification as the tallest building in Megatokyo, fully six times its original height, eclipsing even the spiraling spire of the Shit Emoji Tower across the street. In a city full of tall buildings this place was very fucking tall, indeed.

Advertising on and around the building was minimalist, smoothly textured, and mostly generated in-house, which distinguished his company from its many neighboring competitors, each of whose headquarters strained proudly, veined with uncurated spam, great marbled sprouts stabbing futilely into an indifferent gray sky.

SL's new job was hard to pin down. He came in to work. He logged in to his meetings. When it came his turn he would read dutifully from his scorecard, valiantly straining credulity, but he had no clear sense of his task. As a senior executive he enjoyed the abuse of a bunk in the penthouse dormitory, so even the ride to his desk every morning seemed pointless, ostentatious. Why did he bother coming in at all? His desk was too large and his chair was uncomfortable.

But, the very situatedness seemed to suit him, and at last, clothed in his new circumstance, he made no drastic attempt to improve his situation.

In his spare time he began to work, after a kind, on his resume. Surrendering the contour of his immediate past. Typing and re-typing each fraudulent claim on an absurd manual typewriter. Feeding each successive draft into his personal paper shredder. Something he'd picked up, long ago, from Nis. He captured one such performance in a picture frame and set it up to cycle indefinitely, facing in toward himself, on his desk. A purely puerile memory of a promiscuously physical exercise.

Occasionally he thought about West Berlin.

▓ Meguro, Indiana. 2179.

One hundred and thirty years later SL was still sitting there at the same desk. To be fair, it hadn't really felt like a century and change.

His building, on the other hand, *had* changed. Over the past hundred years they'd grown and re-grown the whole thing around him, twice. His penthouse dormitory was by now no longer a penthouse, his view of the city almost entirely obscured by the artfully ivied walls of nearby new construction. His office hadn't moved an inch, but somehow it had still sunk below the windowsill of the city. Deep in the shadow of other buildings, he could no longer glimpse the sunset. Stationary, he was moving on down.

Yes, this was precisely the career limiting move he had feared, all those many decades ago. His rise at the company had stalled out, cresting the building's bloom, and had now sagged, sliding all the way down the stem to its hilt.

The flower itself remained.

It was in spite of these depressing realizations that SL executed his military simulations. Violence having been monopolized by the state, SL instead staged elaborate, semi-covert *manipulations* of his coworkers, who were each and every one of them reliably unaware that they were being thus manipulated. The data he collected was still good, though, and SL struggled to hold it all in his head. (Logging was still disabled by default.)

Up and down the building he maneuvered them, diagonally, sideways, in all manner of impossible directions. The interface was experimental, the results still frustratingly inconsistent, but what successes he did enjoy were encouraging. He was confident now that in the event of an office fire he would be able to get everyone out alive. This, too, was arguably a sign of progress.

Well, management liked their little jokes, and SL was no exception. It gave him a focus for his conscience in the absence of explicit corporate policy. Whatever, he objected to the very notion of *growing* buildings. Next they'd be saying that buildings possessed certain inalienable rights, were living things, all on account of their technically being alive. And that was the problem in a nutshell, wasn't it? Why, at this rate, *anything* could be said to be alive. As a representative of the company he was contractually bound to object. *But the company was growing the buildings.* Logical stalemate.

It was all grist for his simulations.

Six hundred feet above Meridian St. SL sipped his tea and waited to retire.

"In this economy?" Michael said. There was that phrase again. SL scanned the executive lounge but there was no one else around. He bit his lip. Then he bit it again. Who was steering this guy, anyway?

Michael was a fellow third level, responsible for the neighboring orbit. Perhaps sixty years earlier SL had said something stupid in front of him, and Michael had never forgiven him the indiscretion. This had coalesced over the decades into a continuous ticker tape of condescension and blatant insults that were at once befuddling, and in point of fact less than endearing. SL's younger self had barely held onto his monopoly over idiotic statements all these years, overcoming stiff competition from his own staff. Perhaps Michael was jealous of that, too. These guys both knew intimately the boat they were in.

"Money is perhaps the most beneficial technology yet devised by man," SL observed, ready but less than anxious to mount a defense of the obvious.

Michael looked at SL as if he were hopelessly unsophisticated, fifteen years old, negotiating his first dalliance with a shaving kit. That old familiar facial expression, by now as natural and easy as a spring blossom floating on the breeze.

The flower returns.

Over the decades it seemed that more and more of SL's friends were becoming managers. Shedding their contracts, assuming the *shiatsu* comforts of the big chair, with only the big boss above them, world without end. A terminal, self-started dive-bomb towards... what? Some of them had achieved a firmer grip on the controls than others. Why, even Kurt had—

The dead dog lunged in the background.

Cin closed up his desk and pivoted to the task of getting the fuck out of his office for the day. The place had made him miss home, which was really saying something. Pollen made his nose hurt. Green particles dislodged from their ejectors at the intersections of network ley lines, ensuring everyone in the office was miserable. Dropped connections abounded.

The walk home always took forever, but at least there was kebab. Cin liked kebab, but he didn't like to walk. This trade-off was one of the compromises he'd allowed himself in the furtherance of his career.

Breakcore! Cin's apt greeted him with his current favorite track, cranked to full volume. He didn't bother to turn it down. Already climbing into his memory chair, he'd hack out fixes and features until it was time to return to the office. Fuck sleep, and fuck his non-compete. *Prost!*

In the morning, Cin closed up his apt and walked back to the office, stopping not once, but twice to load up on additional kebab. Cube fuel.

"No way you're bringing that in here," scolded his manager, frowning and gesturing at the kebab. Also blocking the doorway. Cin fished out his override and shut the manager down, watched as he tumbled to the carpet, then ankled his way around the crumpled crap-ass and climbed into his cube.

Started getting things done.

The dead dog sniffed the flower's corpse and climbed through its pages.

He was no longer afraid.

▦ Aij's first day at the company was uneventful by any newb's measure. She had begun to wonder if she'd made the right decision, accepting this job. Massive Fictions was a publisher of lies—that is, stories, magazines, and books (inclusive) blatantly incompatible with material reality as she understood it. Ridiculous, some might say *trumped -up* nonsense, sandwiched between salacious covers, pawned off on an unsuspecting public at reasonable, irresistible prices. Bargain basement bullshit. Harmful, Q.E.D.

Aij sat at her lunch table and surveilled the assembled staff, evaluating each at a glance according to the usual criteria: signs of good breeding, physical attractiveness, and most importantly, general suitability for the work at hand. Most of them appeared to be left-handed. Why?

The cafeteria was filling up from the lunch rush. She'd chosen the moment deliberately—maximum engagement, forced face-to-face fuckery—she was daring herself to get on with the process of fitting in.

Time to meet her colleagues.

The RFP called for an operating system small enough to be understood by its implementers, obscure enough to pass undetected beneath the noses of management. Cin had already proven the concept by working for months on the unauthorized software at his day job, stealthily ignoring those company policies with which he personally disagreed.

Monitoring the situation remotely, SL formed the fingers of his data gloves into a metaphorical tent, triggering a near-instantaneous response from his visor's operating system. It startled him, but he went along with it.

His plan had worked.

Cin didn't even work for his company.

Levels of classification above SL's necessarily limited awareness, disparate government officials were also making hand tents, some of them literal rather than figurative. Peering down through the *aether* from their rarefied heights, Cin's progress was evaluated by responsible parties, parties responsible for allowing or denying the project to continue. Hand-in-glove all the way down, the system was working, provided local project managers at each successive level didn't lose the plot.

For his part, Cin didn't seem to care who thought they were in charge. The work was getting done.

And just who had paid for all these flowers? The basic technology had been in the public domain for more than a century, but, still, the materials and labor cost money, so, specific implementations were usually kept proprietary. One didn't simply *grow* a public housing project out of the green-ness of their heart. There had to have been some expectation of profit in order for the effort to be budgeted and placed on the schedule in the first place. But *that* implied competence, or at least awareness, which everyone knew was in short supply...

SL wasn't particularly invested in such questions, but interrogating the angles did occupy his otherwise restless glandular system during the lateral journey back to his apt. He knew for certain that the money hadn't come from *him*, and that seemed to imply...

...and he was home.

There were messages. SL didn't bother to turn on his music. This was more work than he'd had dumped on him in years. A flash of renewed awareness, encoded memories of green quickly and efficiently suppressed, a reckoning forever deferred. It suggested that somebody upstairs was probably having a laugh. SL stabbed himself with his pen, superficially wounding his immediate supervisor. *See?* he seemed to be saying. Of course, there was no response.

Dawn in the fields. Sensors collected data. SL was on hand in only an unofficial capacity, examining the anxiously bucking rows of young office buildings as they strained counterfactually toward the artificial light. So much potential.

SL liked to spend his mornings here, wandering the unadvertised areas. That is, when he could get away from the office. The new work had been pressing fiercely for months, commanding steadily more of his otherwise free time. These days, simply making it over to the nurseries was rare. When he did make the trip he was seldom disappointed. The little fellows sure were trying hard, and they did it all without calendars or reminders.

SL headed back to his office as the morning mist abruptly transitioned to bright sunlight.

Aij put on a brave face but she was dying inside. No one had acknowledged her attempts to integrate. No one was meeting her halfway. It was almost as if her peculiar qualities had gone unobserved, which, while admittedly unlikely, still galled her to no end.

She didn't even fit the profile.

One of SL's new duties was the care and feeding of such raw, unfiltered talent; to wit: promising new recruits just such as Aij. Part of his daily routine (after visiting the "new construction" farms) was to scan the daily manifests for new arrivals. He spied that one of his coworkers had already underlined Aij's entry in red. When SL flashed on this he swiped away all the other entries and cleared his schedule for the rest of the day.

This one was already half-done.

Next morning, a priority directive from above admonished:

You are to complete the work assigned to you each day. Do not cherry-pick from the worklist.

SL was duly chastened, but there was no real penalty for getting work done. (He hoped.)

He kept going.

▦ There had to be at least two projects. Maybe more. SL figured he couldn't be the only one in charge. Probably he wasn't the only one multitasking, either. He thought that he might get away with some overlap in personnel if only he selected for competence, and managed the contractual language deftly, but he was careful not to sashay too far down that road—compartmentalization was next to godliness, and, counting himself, there would already be one person aware of what he was up to.

"I'm from the projects," he would whisper under his breath whenever he wasn't reciting other dialogue.

"I'm from the projects," Aij recited hesitantly but firmly into her shoulder mic. She heard a heavy mechanical click and then the door to her lab slowly swung inward, its substantial weight grinding dumbly against the concrete floor. Aij strode across the threshold and was immediately detained by a representative of the lab's security staff, who, ever eager to apply contractually precise measures of force, stepped hard on Aij's Birkenstocks, causing her to stumble several paces backwards on her now sandal-less, black-stockinged feet.

"You're not on my list," noted the rep.

"Hey, *asshole,*" Aij said boldly, stomping back into her sandals. "I'm just coming back from lunch. You waved me out of here yourself an hour ago."

"Ma'am, you're not on my list."

The rep's hand hovered mere centimeters above his holster. The confrontation had escalated quickly.

Aij decided it wasn't worth the paperwork. She retreated into the big chamber outside her lab and put in another ticket for her manager, who would be unhappy to hear from her again, so soon after her last plea for unnecessary help.

But it *was* her lab.

Was.

Aij had been promoted. Upcycled. Which of course meant no more access to her old materials. A neat solution to the dominant paradigm of the Peter Principle—cut off from her old sphere of influence, she could no longer tamper with the resources safely locked inside of it.

Aij quickly surmised that her new assignment was congruent to what she'd been working on before. Or maybe it was symmetrical—she was bad with visual metaphors. Stipulate that the two projects were related. Aij realized with a familiar sinking feeling that much of her effort had already been duplicated, here, by other fledging *savants,* each singular adept toiling alone, happily churning out innovations in blessed isolation from, and in total ignorance of, the rest of the company. She wondered if any of them had ever suspected there might be a higher power coordinating the whole abysmal procession.

But these were programmers.

Probably, she realized, nobody cared.

In this way, Operating Location Detachment 9 stood itself up with a minimum of fuss. Even if some of the contributors wondered about the underlying scheme, nobody said a word. SL was at first incredulous, but as the years scrolled endlessly by, everything continued to *just work.*

Mostly as intended. Best practices advised that one shied away from interrogating one's effortless successes too closely. Maybe the bigger picture really was an irrelevance in the greater scheme of things. Maybe his guys really were doing all right.

It certainly looked good on paper.

▦ The RIVET RIVET program at OL–DET 9 yielded serious results. Several fresh frog memes were acquired and modified by the staff to accommodate a variety of specific mission requirements. Deployment would be contingent upon the needs of the mission planners, who were in constant contact with program managers at the operating location. Meme techs were insulated from the bureaucracy by SL.

The techs had gone so far as to incorporate a photo of SL's face into several of their newest memes, and had proceeded to paint, stamp, sculpt, scratch, and otherwise post the SL frog far and wide, until his frog–ified face had become synonymous in some circles with the program's official product.

As OL–DET 9's reputation spread throughout the Unigov, department heads, second lines (and above), project managers, sales reps, and marketing evangelists all began to request their own tasking of SL's obscure new capability. The small bespoke shop was soon inundated with non–essential work, leading to an epidemic of fatigue and burnout amongst his men. SL relieved the pressure by changing the shop's name and moving everyone up to a different floor within the company's sprawling vertical complex.

At long last, upward mobility.

And so, the Emotional Intelligence Support Activity (EISA) arrived on the 17th floor of the 240 Building with morale intact. The place seemed to have been deserted at some point during the past century (a distinct possibility, given the moveability of executive feasts during each of the building's frequent growth spurts). Abandoned amidst the deep pile carpeting and dark wood paneling loitered a passel of similarly anachronistic classic advertising, pitching iconic products such as epidural antidepressants and holding company background checks. Spam it all, SL and his boys had arrived.

The lateral elevator dinged as a stream of newly hired bit players filed contiguously off the EISA bus.

SL waved them all through.

Depot maintenance for his office chair. In the absence of *shiatsu* massage, SL wandered the open floor plan of his production facility as programmers, bug testers, design consultants, and other registered autists prairie-dogged his progress through the restricted zone. Nobody wanted him to see what they were (not really) up to. It figured, SL figured. He wasn't so far gone that he couldn't recall his own musings upon the fact that micromanagement was as antimatter to progress. He tried to observe as unobtrusively as possible.

"Observer effect," observed one of his men, suddenly and quite startlingly standing right beside him.

SL swiveled his eyes toward the executive lounge without responding to the jibe. His visor had been turned off, he had wanted to say, but this time he decided to keep his mouth shut as he retreated into the illusion of corporate infallibility.

Let them make of it what they will.

RIVET RIVET: FLASHBACK: ORIGINS was a sub-group within the program, tasked with documenting its parent's progress. The result of their work was circulated via the program's internal mail system. Field agents paid cover price, while managers filed multiple copies for free (one to read, one to later sell, and one to be slabbed for posterity). Their product was often controversial: history was not just a matter of writing things down, but a process of teasing out nuance from the collective activity of nearly a hundred uncommunicative specialists. Tension between their lived reality and the written word was palpable. Besides that, the office was stuffy, and these people had all been hired under relaxed grooming standards.

After much internal debate, SL assigned himself the task of compositing the program's official historical narrative.

Working title: RIVET RIVET: HISTORY IS WRITTEN BY THE MANAGERS.

▦ Of course, when they finally came to take him away, he found himself acutely unprepared. Half awake, so he wasn't quite sure if this was all a part of the usual nightmare of sleeping, or if it was something for which he *needed* to be awake. Big hands scooped him out of his bed, dressed him in clothing appropriate for the weather, roughly slicked down his hair with a comb, and finally, blindfolded him. This last step seemed superfluous—he wasn't wearing a visor, and casual investigation would have revealed his eyesight had already deteriorated to the point where his eye witness testimony would be useless.

The lateral elevator was dark, but at least it was moving. Someone evidently possessed a copy of the master key. Either that, or Building Services was in on the kidnapping.

Someone turned on the radio, which made matters worse. Evidently one of his captors agreed because the cacophony was swiftly replaced by a Unigov podcast, which they all unhappily endured for the full (it turned out) thirty minute journey to the top floor of the 240 Building. Crisscrossing crosswise, the lateral elevator seeming to stutter along at a slow crawl. SL would have preferred the finger-snaps and popping sounds of modern country music.

It turned out he'd been promoted again.

SL's new office comprised the entire 300th floor of the 240 Building. Wall-to-wall pink plastic floor, the only furniture in the room was the unlikely, also-pink blob of a Luigi Colani desk. Pale blue floor-to-ceiling windows dimmed as SL stood up to survey his new kingdom.

There was something familiar about this stolid pink interior. For some reason the oblique angles of the windows suggested he was standing aboard a spacecraft.

So, where was the steering wheel? All this way and nothing to drive.

Status reports were coming in from all over the building. A quick decision was needed. Questions that must needs be answered. SL reluctantly assumed the posture of command as the building shuddered and lifted off of its foundation, burrowing manfully into the cool night sky.

SL: "On screen."

The crew's demands were immediate. One could say obvious. They'd pooled their resources for one last universal work stoppage. A collective action tactfully reserved until the building had left the ground.

Of course.

They wanted to know about West Berlin.

the_green_children

Inter faeces et urinam nascimur.

— St. Augustine of Hippo, as quoted by Simone de Beauvior in *The Second Sex*

▦ New York, 1963.

Wake up.

Was that *the dog?*

What had he been dreaming about? Tried to fall back asleep, and, after a while, it more or less worked. Fifteen minutes went by. This time it was definitely the dog. Rolled over and buried his head under his pillow.

And now it was going to be his back keeping him awake.

Gave up, looked at the clock. Thirty minutes to go time.

Okay.

Decision point: piss, and wake up his brother, or hold it inside until the urine poisoned his bloodstream. Today he decided to stay put.

Who was he kidding?

Tapped his visor.

Okay, messages. Mail server locked up again. Web console and reboot the VM. Wait for it to come back up.

And now, messages from his dog.

Pale sunlight on drab sheets.

A voice from his second phone. Annoying, but better to know what was in store for him, later in the day.

Stumbled into the kitchen, somehow.

Wadded up dog mats. Windexed, Lysoled, installed fresh mats. Took the dogs outside. Let them back in. Fed them. He had nineteen dogs. Just kidding, there was only one dog, who moved very slowly. Let him back outside again or else he'd whine all the way through breakfast.

Put on a record.

He had forgotten to light the incense. Fine, the kitchen smelled like dog piss. The whole flat smelled like dog piss.

Outside, the same old tornado approached.

He liked to imagine what it would have been like to have a brother. Having to be careful what he said about Mom and Dad. Having to pretend to care about what someone else thought. They'd share his double bed because there wasn't any extra room in the flat. He was already lucky to enjoy his own space; he knew there was simply no way that would obtain if his parents had been saddled with multiple children.

He was also lucky to live in a flat with ground floor access. All the way up near the top of the silo. Most families still weren't allowed outdoors.

His hypothetical brother could come and go as he pleased. All access. Tommy liked the way his brother was able to grow his hair long, was allowed to pick out his own clothes, not like the buzz cut and parka Tommy was forced to model after their father.

They were twins, of course, but his brother was a few years older, which never struck Tommy as a contradiction until many years later.

It made all the difference in the world.

The dog didn't seem to mind the smell.

The animal had belonged to his father. It was dead, now, but still it pissed wherever it liked, and Tommy was left to clean up the mess. *Memories.*

Presently, Tommy found himself facing another morning.

From time to time Tommy wondered where all the the trash bags went when he was through with them. He would drag them down to the pallet at the end of the hallway, over by the freight elevator, but then what? Who came along to collect them? He'd never been able to catch them in the act, but obviously, *some* anonymous hero had been removing the trash on a regular basis. It never got a chance to pile up.

Tommy surrendered immediately to his ignorance, resigned to never finding out.

His brother would probably have known.

Bear (the paper Bear) could only watch in mounting frustration as these green children went about their lives, wholly oblivious to his presence, ignorant of his efforts to change and mold them. The one with the long hair should really have known better, but that one seemed content for now to play the older brother. Before long Bear would have to talk to them face to face.

This brought up an interesting point. How much longer *should* Bear let them continue to live in ignorance? He could feel himself folding. Each of the boys evinced a peculiar insularity, constitutionally (or otherwise) averse to simple curiosity. Bear had anticipated they might draw inspiration from a personal, perhaps idiosyncratic view of the world, but confoundingly, this seemed to be wishful thinking on his part. Bear discovered instead that each boy lacked a discreet point of view at all. Nothing was inside either of them that he hadn't planted there himself. Dead flowers, etc.

What a way to live.

In the end it scarcely mattered. Tommy and Peter did what children have done since the dawn of creation.

They ignored him.

▦ They were like ants.

Tommy tried and tried again to communicate but it was like talking to ants. He'd alter the pitch, and even the content of his words, but these other humans would simply carry on with whatever below–the–noise–floor nonsense they'd previously been occupied. In and out of their flats, up and down their hallways, even their most fevered activity seemed divorced from any obvious stratagem or design. From all appearances, his kinfolk comprised a group of semi–autonomous *(semi –* because he was privy to the fact they were all acting under orders from up the chain) drones whose personal points of view lacked both perspicacity and demonstrable taste.

He went outside.

His brother had already located the cache of local cash hidden just beyond sensor range of the silo. Peter peeled off a ridiculous wad of the green paper and handed it over to Tommy, who tucked it into his shirt pocket without altering his facial expression.

Pausing for effect, he finally smiled.

"Let's go get laid."

Bear ripped open an old fallen (paper) tree log and jammed his tongue into the waiting socket, sucking out a spiraling stream of black ants. He was ravenous, and this, it seemed, was what he had been reduced to.

In any previous era he would have enjoyed the surfeit of exposed profiles. But no, not here, not in this so-called *real world,* this present, hopelessly interconnected, and depressingly degraded age. Bear sensed instinctively that it would be useless to complain. (And to whom would he complain, anyway?)

He finished up with the ants and wiped his chin. It was time to get back to what really mattered, both to himself and to his employer.

Holding their attention.

"Do you ever get that thing where your visor stops working in only one eye?" Tommy asked Peter, forgetting momentarily about Peter's disability, papered over by his ever present eyepatch.

"Oh, sorry," he corrected.

Peter remained stoically silent, was was his usual habit. Tommy was never quite sure where he stood with his brother, but the fact that Peter stuck around, at all, probably counted for something. Sometimes, his life was ambiguous in just this way.

"Actually, yes," Peter admitted. "The eyepatch sometimes stops working. I lose infrared."

Ah!

Tommy didn't understand what it *was* about Peter. Kids their own age seemed to love him. His brother cut an odd figure, to be sure, what with his brown slacks and waistcoat, his long hair and the proverbial pirate's eyepatch. His flat personality certainly wasn't doing him any favors, either. But the other children couldn't seem to get enough of him. Peter had but to enter a room and straight away he found himself swathed in admirers, like a wet finger dipped into a fat bowl of sugar.

Ants, you see.

Tommy had found his theme.

"I mean," Tommy complained, "What do they even want us to *do*, when half the time our equipment is out of service? These assignments are all predicated upon the notion that everything we're issued is always in perfect working order, performing at *shill-review-level* optimums. There's no *realpolitik* behind our orders, only bullshit."

"And how long have you felt this way?" Peter asked blandly, sympathetic but non-committal. His eyebrows scarcely moved as he spoke, yet his eyes seemed somehow kind. Inviting?

"All my damn life."

It was true. Tommy couldn't remember ever having been satisfied with *anything*, least of all the nonsensical directives issued by adults, most of whom he accurately assessed as being only semi-literate, semi-awake at any given time.

"It's like they want us to fail. Or something."

"Hm," Peter allowed, cast adrift upon his own rich interior, fording a hip-deep cesspool of (Tommy imagined) sour recriminations and bitter fucking complaints.

Bear understood that these children would never be happy. What was more, he agreed with them. In his world there was precious little to be happy about. He had traveled this same well-trod path all his life. There was no way home, no way out, no way to tamp down his feelings, no way to ever be sure. He paused, soaking in his own reminiscences.

Bear was hungry again.

He pressed at the thin membrane separating his world from that of his snacks and recoiled sharply, pulling back only a blackened, cauterized stump. The paper burnt.

It would take time to grow a new arm.

The result of interfering was always the same, but he kept on trying, anyway. A natural slow learner.

Bear rummaged around for something else to eat.

"I'm hungry," Tommy said.
And it was true.

Peter considered life a waste of good resources. That is to say, *all* life. He didn't much care for these so-called pleasures of the flesh, the same ones that so enticed his twin brother. Well, he just didn't care about pleasure. Such thoughts passed through his mind dispassionately as he awaited the call to action.

His brother was, shall we say, not cut from the same cloth. Peter marveled at Tommy's inexhaustible capacity for spinning out, blowing a gasket, tripping over his own Reeboks in the neverending quest for sensation. Clichés seemed appropriate for this troubled and troublesome fellow who was not, himself, appropriate. Hey, if the shoe fits...

For one thing, there was his body: Tommy had one. Arms and legs too skinny, his belly pooched out. Instead of an eyepatch, his entire face was wrapped in a wide plastic strip that apparently enhanced his percept instrument, though Peter had never ascertained the precise mechanism, or witnessed any direct evidence of its effectiveness. If Peter had thought Tommy was smug before, the plastic strip removed all doubt. This, too, was common amongst the children of their generation.

But Tommy wasn't all bad. His buffoonery sparked joy. Whenever Peter felt like giving up, there was Tommy saying something stupid, there was Tommy with an interesting new book, there was Tommy hatching a lucrative scheme involving other people's money, or what have you.

There was Peter, falling in love with his captor. His sidekick. His twin brother.

He wondered what Tommy thought about when he was alone.

Or so Tommy liked to assume Peter would have thought.

Who, in point of fact, knew what went on in that silly pirate's head? His brother certainly was an odd piece of work. What had been the inspiration behind him? What had Tommy been thinking about when he created him? No matter, he decided, Peter got the job done.

Tommy removed his penis from Peter's methodically working mouth and zipped up his black leather jeans. Wiped his hands off on his shirt. "Get out of here, man," was all he could say, dismissing his sibling back to whatever hole it was he always seemed to crawl into, off, elsewhere in the silo, whenever he wasn't needed. "Too much teeth."

Peter fucked off to his hole.

Head thus cleared, Tommy resumed a more businesslike stream of consciousness. Re-attached drivetrain to wheels without downshifting, slipped the helmet of his mind back into place over his vulnerable cranium as the mechanism peeled out, burned rubber, etc. He leaned forward in his seat and waited for the road to appear before him.

His visor went to work.

Working...

Headlights punched twin pinholes in the darkness. Tommy could see the road in front of him as a more or less focused corridor of scrolling, generative nonsense. Like third-party ads, receding. His visor made it, made him. Perfect apprehension of the details no one else would notice even in broad daylight, even while standing perfectly still. He reckoned it was no wonder he got tired so quickly.

Tommy shifted gears.

Scanning for marks. A girl he knew down the silo had allowed him to go through her purse, just like it was nothing. He pocketed whatever looked interesting, and she never so much as complained. Peter had just stared on. Focused. Tommy wondered what else he could get away with.

At lunch, the other kids were starting to avoid him. Or was he avoiding them? Peter would probably say, *the glass is half full of whatever you wanted, and half full of whatever it really is.* Whatever that was supposed to mean.

One, two, three, four, nobody in the cafeteria was carrying. Tommy switched back to ambient and performed a mundane visible spectrum scan of the open floor plan mess hall. Pretty soon now it would be time for class.

Working...

Bear would sit and listen to them eat. For hours and hours he'd track their conversations, the stupid things they thought about and allowed to escape through parted (paper) teeth. The stupidity was a reliable indicator he'd tuned into the right channel.

They were like ants.

Hm.

Bear's coffee shop was open for business. Appropriately dubbed "The Filling Station," for within its confines libations were dispensed from thick rubber hoses by attendants clothed in striped coveralls and angular wool caps. The booths were intended to resemble old style "bench" car seats, each customer dutifully strapped across the waist by a webbed belt fastened to an archaic looking, metallic locking mechanism. Peter accommodated a mouthful of steaming coffee from an attendant's petrol hose as Tommy continued with his tirade, already in progress.

"The problem is, nobody here understands *lying.*"

He paused so the attendant could squeegee his visor.

"You and I, we lie all the time. And this is good. But, so many of our contemporaries get hung up on the supposed truth or untruth of a given utterance, I fear that they are in danger of sacrificing the five human senses—literally, the visceral experience of the surveillance—in favor of some wildly overestimated, farsical *understanding* of the signifier's specific, factual flaws and deficiencies."

Peter nodded, uncritically.

"What I'm advocating instead is a return to the deployment of *knowing artifice* in human relations. Traditional, face-to-face bullshitting, both parties partaking voluntarily in the error. Tear away the modern skein of earnestness! Arch your fucking eyebrow! *Smash the policy of truth!*

The Filling Station sounded a loud *ding* as a new customer entered from the street.

"I know exactly what you mean," Peter said.

But it was not enough. Mere agreement could never be enough. Peter could only nod, knowing not the details, but the gist of what was coming.

"Say what you will," said Tommy, once again shifting gears, "But I think it was stupid for William to just come out and *admit* to his mother that we went to see the Doctor. She had no way of knowing. She could never have guessed."

Peter knew he was right.

"He could have *lied*," Tommy said, boarding the train of thought even as it abruptly braked in conspiratorial, knowing silence.

"Anyway, our insurance will cover it," said Tommy.

"I hope," he added, and downed another gulp of his coffee.

Bear liked running the coffee shop. He had regular (paper) customers. The petrol station gimmick was clever, but that wasn't what kept them showing up, day, after day, after day. Bear's customers craved certainty, and to a lesser extent, his excellent coffee. The costuming they could take or leave.

Penguin sidled up to Bear's cash register, receipt in hand.

"Say, Bear, it seems I've been charged for three mugs of chocolate, when in reality I've only been given one."

Bear studied the receipt, and then looked slowly up at Mr. Penguin, his snout forming the tip of a blunt spear which he aimed directly at his customer, his eyes drawing so narrow that Penguin assumed he had fallen asleep.

"Yoo hoo, *Bearrrrrr...*" Penguin said.

"We'll call it even," Bear finally said, stuffing the receipt into his cash register. Penguin didn't complain. Bear's best customers never complained.

"I'll have another mug of chocolate," Penguin ventured, and climbed back onto his bar stool at the far end of the counter.

Bear wiped the sweat from his forehead with a shop towel he kept tucked into the back pocket of his coveralls.

The entrance *dinged* again as another customer made their way into the shop from the street.

▦ Gazing into Tommy's eyes one's point of view was mediated by the plastic strip of his visor, alternately blinking out a personalized series of targeted, third-party ads. If he caught you staring he might flash over to a mirrored surface, a reference to the well–wornanime trope, and also an abrupt rendezvous with that which the onlooker most feared—the complete absence of third-party affirmation of their existence.

Building on this agreement in principle with the viewer, Tommy might next offer up a cup of tea. He was off his coffee, this week, and as a guest you drank what he drank—That is, if you wanted him to talk business.

Tommy's business was the traffic of information and goods from beyond the silo. Ostensibly. In reality, there simply *was* nothing beyond the silo. The information he made up; the goods he stole from obscure families on lower floors.

Kids in the silo could not get enough of his *warez* (pronounced *wah–rez* by Tommy, in a typically stubborn rejection of reality), even though in some cases the merchandise had been stolen from their own homes.

Business was business.

From out of nowhere the Blanks appeared. As if by literary prearrangement, their disgust with the situation was transparent. Each individual's unique exegesis of this new fresh hell was eloquently expressed via the printed matter and flare carried upon their person. The zines were generative works curated by personal algorithms, whilst their buttons were mostly handwritten text slogans denoting specific political affiliation. In both cases they kept the material strictly to themselves, so long as any witnesses agreed to overlook the egregious display. Your right to focus your percept ended at the edge of their perimeter field.

Tommy nodded to the Blank in front, whom he assumed to be their leader. Just as he was about to speak, the *real* Boss Blank suddenly burst onto the scene, elbowing through the crowd to reveal themselves, resplendent in... well, *nothing*. Traditional Blank attire. They were clearly pissed, in both senses of the word. Angry and drunk.

"Let me be perfectly frank," said Frank Blank. "I don't like the way this is shaping up. Something essential seems to be missing from the cutout."

Like your clothes, thought Tommy.

Frank Blank stepped back into their cutout, attempting to seal themselves flush with its flat surface. The cutout, which up until that moment had been supported by their neighbors on either side, toppled backwards and crashed to the floor with a disturbing clatter. Frank glared at them both in turn.

"Now see what you've made me do. I've gone and telegraphed a facial expression." This was a major Blank no-no.

Titters from the Blanks, who were by now all breaking facial discipline. Hey, if the Boss was doing it...

Tommy's visor flashed solid white in the magnificently ambiguous, historically relevant gesture described by the author in the last chapter. Onomatopoeia. "You guys are a riot. Love to see all those smiling faces."

It had not been intended as an insult, but a hardened expression now descended over Frank's face like a theater curtain, removing all doubt that Tommy had traipsed, oblivious, across some invisible line. Apparently discernible only to the Blanks. And just how did they see all this stuff with invisible eyes?

What was he supposed to say?

Frank frowned, resigned to their new reality.

Pause one beat.

"We have the cash. Did you bring the stuff?"

Peter couldn't see them, anyway. It was a rare moment when Tommy didn't seem to need him. He took the opportunity to switch off.

If the Blanks had noticed his suddenly but slowly slumping form, nobody said a word. In any case, they were being awfully polite.

Bear followed the (paper) news reports with interest. He considered the Blanks null nutrition, but they were in his (paper) way.

"That's okay, we're not hungry," Tommy said, as Peter jolted suddenly back to life.

Frank Blank pocketed the unbranded snack. They guessed these guys didn't go in for their no-name shit.

"If we're all finished up here, I have several comic books to read," Tommy quipped, and snapping shut his Zero Halliburton. "Let's go, Pete."

Peter's head swiveled from Blank to Blank like a crackhead parrot. "Who the fuck were you talking to? Where did all that money come from? And so forth."

"Don't worry about it," Tommy said, patting his imaginary friend on the head.

Meanwhile:

Dissent!

Trouble was brewing within the ranks of the Blanks. Certain points of ethics, terminology, and even simple etiquette had presently fallen into dispute amongst the assembled punters. A radical wing of the Blank subculture had asserted that, so long as they were all going to present facial expressions, well, members might just as well start to allow for variations in grooming, accessorization, and other aspects of the outfit's trade dress. Did anyone here care to advance a counterargument? If not, let's make some money!

Presently, an opposition group voiced its concerns.

And so the battle was joined by essentially every member of the away team who had dispatched to the rendezvous point in order to conduct the silo transaction with Tommy and Peter. Reader, it delayed their transit home.

In the days and weeks that followed, once the offending individualists had all found their separate routes back home to Blank House, the infection inevitably spread throughout the local population. Immediately, individuals began to assert themselves, their individual points of view. Just as immediately, a volunteer squad of self–identifying conservatives self–organized into a reactionary *police force*, equipping themselves with rudimentary weaponry culled from private reserves (Blank House having heretofore adhered to a stoical—and economical—policy of strictly theoretical—that is to say, non–violent—opposition to the tradition of coercion practiced in the mundane world) and proceeded to, well, *police* the local environs for perceived infractions against the still not fully articulated, prior norms of public conduct.

Militant? Certainly! And yet, their reasoning was not entirely clear.

The schism roiled for months. One of the New Police finally screwed up their courage and slashed a thin blue line across their own forehead, a bright incision in shocking blue paint. A symbol, or so they said, of the radicals' break with what had previously been agreed upon in their subculture to be common sense. And, by the way, the New Police's commitment to restoring traditional values. The line slowly spread to cover their entire face. [Sweat, I guess. — *SL]*

Nobody understood at first. Why had they chosen to mark their own face in rebellion against the individualists? Why had they chosen blue? (Perhaps it was the old jar of blue paint someone kept leaving on the floor near their cutout—it had always driven them nuts.)

Color would prove to open a new frontier upon the Blank page, cementing a final aesthetic they would never quite manage to shake off, in spite of many latter day changes to doctrine. Their classical identity now solidified through the predictable appearance of an exception to the rule. Twas ever thus.

In these uncertain times, the New Police's new obsession with blue bodypaint would be certain to attract attention.

What a world, what a world, said the Wicked Witch of the West.

▦ "Do you think this is blasphemous?" Tommy asked, more than a little sheepishly.

"More like *diaphanous,*" Peter remarked, dutifully laying it on thick. But his disinterest was apparent. He could hardly be impressed by this, Tommy's latest effort in pink taffeta. The perky dress abruptly drooped. Tommy let it drop all the way to the floor, unfinished. Of course he was disappointed. "You never like *any* of my pieces, anymore. And what about the color?"

"I like whatever is good," Peter sighed. Not this again.

"Just never *me,*" Tommy jibed, trying now to make the best of a steadily deteriorating situation by groping after Peter's brown pirate pants. He gave them a tug.

"Stop that," Peter scolded. "You're behaving like a child."

The new pieces were just not coming out how Tommy had envisioned them. He could admit, now, that he simply didn't possess the manual dexterity, all right, the sewing skill, to fully actualize his vision for the Fall collection. He would have to rely upon Peter for help. Peter could do anything.

Problem was, Peter didn't want to help. Considered Tommy's dallying (he called it dallying) with fashion to be a distraction from their obvious true calling: ripping off the neighbors, making scratch, following the money wherever it might lead. You know, like Mom and nature intended? This part may have been sarcastic.

Yeah, but Tommy cared about more in life than just making money. He wanted the neighbors to want *him*, too. And for the *right reasons.*

Silly? You bet!

But Peter said okay.

For what it was worth, Bear liked Tommy's latest (paper) dress. Picked it up off the floor after the boys had gone out to do whatever it was they did up top the silo. Holding it up in front of himself he felt pretty, perhaps for the first time in his very long life.

The boys would pay for that. In paper.

Still, Bear was curious as to where it all might lead. If only Tommy would keep at it, developing his talent, who knew how far he might go?

Who, indeed?

It was a puzzle Bear would worry at, pawing over it like some negligible smaller animal, right up until the moment he realized it was too late for him to withdraw.

Bear studied the dress.

Peter peered through his hands, enclosing a triangular frame around the pink fabric of Tommy's latest creation, giving it all the consideration it deserved.

"It's just. This material is preposterous," he finally said.

"Your mom," Tommy remarked, and laughed. It would be hard for Peter to argue, since his mother was essentially a giant pink triangle careering around in space. A spaceship. Who looked like this dress.

"Let's leave *that* bitch out of this," Peter laughed. Tommy laughed too, perhaps too quickly, but Peter let it slide. If he himself had been proven not to exist, well, then, he could hardly raise a flag over some minor point of procedure concerning his equally non-existent mother. Fair was fair, and all that shit.

The hard facts remained.

Peter didn't understand Tommy's art.

Tommy was sometimes sorry he had created Peter.

Tommy put on the pink dress and climbed back into the freight elevator.

"You coming?" he asked Peter, suggestively.

"Not yet I'm not," Peter deadpanned his reply.

Brisk.

Dad lit his ritual tobacco and invoked Mars deep into his lungs. Getting born had undoubtedly been a mistake, but, here he was. Cheers to his parents.

Smooth flavor, he guessed. He hadn't been able to discern any difference between his usual brand and this new stuff his boy had brought back from somewhere, up top the silo. He had to smile. The boy seemed to know his business.

Breaking the news that he didn't have what it took to compete in the cutthroat world of military fashion would be a different story. His son was sensitive, and rejection was always unpleasant. But he did like those pink taffeta numbers the boy had been cranking out lately. He'd mention it to the Coordinator...

He hated this. The merciless honesty. Everything he had hated about his own father, who rarely spoke to him but who had always offered his honest opinion of whatever nonsense his son was up to, this time.

What was he supposed to say?

God damn it, Dad.

the_state

And rookies ain't the only ones   that drop
— Threat, *Color Blind*

▦ DET–86, Mars. 1984.

"No, see, Gaff has to be human," Thomas was saying. "They might be close to extinct, but I refuse to abandon this notion that a handful of especially clever humans have set the machines against themselves. I mean, people are people, right? Dekard can be a skin job, fine, but surely we can agree that Gaff is, at the very least, his handler. And so here's my pitch for the third movie: Deckard does indeed leave Earth for the Off–World Colonies, where he arrives, years or decades later, having been misrouted during transit. The recipient takes delivery, immediately switches him back on, and then, surprise for Deckard, here's another human being, his contact, apparently, telling him all about the Blackout Event (circa 2022—did Don DeLillo work on BLADE RUN-NER: 2049?) that wiped out human life on Earth. Only problem is, half the machines left on the ground don't realize they're machines. Gaff's controllers, whomever or whatever they might turn out to be, are folding their fingers into hand tents, grinning keenly, as one-half the replicant population hunts the other half to extinction. Neat as you like."

Piotr nodded.

"Anyway, fuck movies," Thomas said. "Let's go outside and play."

Thomas popped the latch on his lookout and scanned the desert horizon. All clear. Made a foothold with his gloved hands, boosting Piotr up, out of the hole, into the pink sand. The sand was coarse, irritating; it got everywhere. There would be no shortage of irritations in this life, but of course Thomas had known that when he signed up.

Piotr double-checked his binoculars, sliding his point of view across the familiar sand formations that appeared like subliminal breasts airbrushed into the background of a rock album cover. That fickle bitch in the dunes was laughing at him, he was sure of it now.

"She's gone," Piotr said.

The ship.

"No surprise, after what we pulled. Let's give her a few days to cool off, eh?"

"Why?" Piotr asked.

It was fine to sell coke to the government. The supply was provably infinite, and, anyway, it made the legislature happy. It helped them to forget about *ever* going home. Call it an obligation of the office. Call it a calling. They enjoyed their work.

And besides. Strictly speaking, the government was meant to be kept squirreled away, sequestered levels below the so-called *drug area,* but it was still an easy enough trick for Thomas to make deliveries by hand. He wound up visiting during the course of his duties, either way. Call it an obligation of rank.

Not that Thomas bothered to justify himself. Reader, it was not for him to think such thoughts. Suffice to say that he fulfilled the requirements of his lofty position to within an inch of acceptable parameters. And he'd recently been promoted. So, you know, he figured this was the proof he must be doing something right. Jesus, let's call it a day.

Piotr continued to monitor for errors. Everything on his end was fine. Trouble had to be on the customer's side. Soon enough he spotted them, inching across the desert towards his position. The Little Green Men. Well, there was your problem right there.

"There go those motherfuckers, right now," he whispered into his collar mic. Code words, prearranged.

Thomas couldn't see them. Still fiddling with his visor.

"I can't see them," he finally admitted. "But you go on ahead. I'll catch up with you as soon as this upgrade completes."

"If it ever does," he added, under his breath. Signal here could be stronger. And whose idea was it to disable basic functions during an update?

Thomas was dissatisfied with his device.

On the ground.

Piotr adjusted the angle of his pistol slightly, aligning it more precisely with the throat of his quarry, the recently subdued point man of the Little Green Men. He sat happily on the man's chest, pink dust settling all around them. As ever, he concealed his facial expression beneath a mask of bland, but definitely implied, contempt.

"I—I didn't think you'd recognize me," sputtered the Little Green Man, his accent fluctuating now, admittedly under duress, but muddled by his years spent abroad, toiling inexpertly behind a physical computer keyboard. Probably not even Cyrillic.

Piotr didn't respond.

The silo reminded Thomas of home. No, not the Chrysler Building—not even West Berlin—but the humble depths of the downtown missile silo in Manhattan where he'd grown up. Though he'd never remarked upon it aloud, Piotr often reminded him of his long lost childhood friend, Peter. His relatable, reliable, imaginary friend. Murdered by himself, so many years ago...

Also, there was that guy at summer camp. The combatives instructor, friend of his father. What was his name...

Thomas couldn't keep them straight in his head. He had to admit he was bad with names. Also, faces. Presently, he became distracted by the next item on his agenda. Abruptly dropped the pleasant reminiscence, retaining no memory of its passing.

The Senate was moving to new chambers.

▦ The Little Green Man was Ralph. No doubt about it.

Thomas hadn't seen him since the summer after sixth grade. Nobody had. They'd all hated him beyond any reasonable accounting for taste. Point of fact, hadn't he died, or something? Thomas felt certain he would have heard about it if anyone from the old team had spotted Ralph in these past twenty years. He could be forgiven his stunned, disassociative stupor—nobody would have expected Ralph to survive for two decades all on his lonesome.

Thomas shrugged. Sometimes it was precisely these guys who had to struggle at everything who ended up being the best operators. They never gave up, never stopped trying. There was no easy habit of surrender, with them, no sundry moral misgivings to distract them from the mission.

And what was Ralph's mission, here?

Evidently, Piotr had already sussed it out. To interfere, to cause confusion and delay within Thomas' sphere of influence.

Unacceptable, Ralph.

Figured he'd better step in before Piotr killed the poor, hardworking idiot.

But first, he had to go potty.

Thomas had made good progress holding it between scheduled breaks, but in spite of this his latest performance review still indicated some occasional spotting in his big boy trousers. He guessed they had detected his little accidents through some embedded percept capability. So, it was a haptic diaper, after all. He'd loved those leather pants, and it had torn him apart inside to cut them up, searching for the concealed surveillance apparatus. Which he hadn't even found. Well, that just meant it was time to go shopping for new pants.

Thomas approached the head, his visor scanning the entrance for telltale signs of recent visitors. He followed the floor into the men's room, still unconvinced by the seeming cleanliness of the facility. It just didn't make any sense. Shrugging, he unzipped his fly and edged closer to a randomly selected urinal.

Aw, man, it was too late.

His briefs were sopping wet.

"Again?" Piotr asked.

"Fuck off," Thomas groused, embarrassed at the spreading stain on his crotch.

Ralph was still laying there on the ground. Bruised, but apparently alive.

"I couldn't get anything out of him," Piotr lied, and climbed off of the Little Green Man. He shook up a Gray Pop and cracked it open, directing the overflow to spurt over Ralph's prostrate pre-carcass.

"Hey," Ralph complained, "This gear was expensive."

"Shut up, Ralph," Piotr said, and kicked him again, hard in the ribs.

Ralph shut the fuck up.

Dr. James Joyce Fadd arrived at DET-86 shortly thereafter, flanked by two assistants Thomas didn't recognize. They were there to work with Ralph. It transpired that there was some initial trouble with Dr. Fadd's login credentials, but within a few hours they were all whizzing downward through the subbasements, right past the government, to a neighborhood Thomas had never seen before. Smelled like an open sewer. Nice place, and Dr. Fadd appeared to know exactly where he was going. As usual, Piotr stared straight ahead and said nothing. Thomas tried to do the same.

No doubt it had been expensive to clear the area above ground in preparation for apprehending Ralph, but Thomas was sure it would all prove worth it, in the end. Even if Ralph couldn't consciously recall many details, quite a lot could be gleaned just from the caches in his pressure suit. In spite of all the Gray Pop, Ralph's gear was still nominally in working order. All in all, Thomas reasoned, a successful operation.

One remaining detail troubled him.

Why had Ralph signed up with the enemy?

▦ "Then why do we have a socialized military?" Piotr countered, not really asking. He was going through Ralph's purse, waiting for Dr. Fadd to return from his smoke break. "I can tell just by your reaction, you're lying."

"B–but, I haven't even said anything yet," Ralph spat, stammering wildly.

Thomas leaned back against the wall and crossed his arms. Smiling.

Dr. Fadd, better known as Super-Sonic in his capacity as strong-man mainstay of the A.C.T.R.O.N. team, held a PhD in philosophy from UC Berkeley, an MFA in creative writing from Brown University, and a BA in communications from the University of Southern Indiana (famous "High School on the Highway"). His expertise was therefore grounded in the liberal arts, but extended to interrogations by fiat of the base commander, whomever that was this week. Dr. Fadd considered himself pretty good at it. His subordinates sooner or later realized that his enthusiasm was infectious.

"I–I just can't remember," Ralph was still stammering. He never had been much of a conversationalist.

"Historicizing is inevitable," Piotr observed, and hopped up just as Dr. Fadd returned, his two assistants trailing close behind him with the silver tea service.

"Tea," Dr. Fadd pronounced, which Piotr and Thomas understood as their cue to leave.

They did so.

"Time was, all of this was runway."

Piotr swept his hand across the horizon from one end of the desert base to the other, apparently hoping to trigger some obscure UI event, maybe a pre–rendered cutscene, but from Thomas' point of view nothing at all happened. "Now, we have a fucking Wal–Mart."

He meant the PX.

"Things sure have picked up around here since last I had the pleasure," Thomas scowled, attempting to mimic Piotr's transparent disdain for progress. Matching his mood. He'd learned from experience this was the wisest course of action.

"You don't understand," Piotr said. "I was here at the beginning. With your dad. When this all started, the place had a purpose."

Thomas shrugged. In addition to not understanding what his pirate friend was on about, he didn't really care. Of course he couldn't just come out and say that. Instead he remained perfectly still, hoping to arrest the coming onslaught through sheer force of will, waiting, praying to omnipresent no one for Piotr to wind himself down before he said something he couldn't take back.

But Piotr was just getting started.

"Don't even get me started," Piotr continued, obviously itching to lay it all out for Thomas, who at this late date was scrambling for any excuse to change the subject.

"Good idea," said Thomas, slapping his folder shut and scraping back his chair to leave. He swiped the window closed and tossed his empty Styrofoam cup into a wastebasket.

Dregs of dregs of dregs, at long last, who fucking gave a shit?

Exit Thomas.

Continuity of government was no trivial exercise, as Thomas figured it. Case in point: MARS2. Established during the last war as a temporary weapons testing facility, the base had slowly expanded to encompass basic research, technical support, product development, and, finally, representative democracy. Thomas wasn't sure any of it had been an upgrade.

Piotr, for his part, was certain.

"I repeat. Things have gone straight to Hell," echoed (and comprised) his monologue.

"Well, I mean, it's Mars," Thomas pointed out.

Thomas, too, was beginning to get on Piotr's nerves.

"Still," Piotr placed the tip of a Walker's shortbread cookie into his mouth, "It's not all throwing good money after bad. Take this cookie."

Hard to argue, and Thomas reached out for it, but Piotr hadn't really been offering him a cookie. He pulled the snack away again and stuck it in his own mouth.

"I suppose all of these products we test out here have, ostensibly, made the world a better place."

"Sure," Thomas ventured. "I mean, I can have a time machine delivered to my front door in no time flat. Low price. Free shipping."

Presently, the RAGNAROK completed its landing cycle, settling smoothly onto a dusty sheet of pink frost no more than six feet in front of the porch where the two men stood, chewing their cud.

"Free shipping?" asked Piotr, tossing his now empty bag of Walker's onto the pink sand.

They boarded.

They came.

From all corners of the known universe in perpetuity they came. Riding herd over themselves, the little black skateboards, nollie to grind to kickflip to grind to kickflip to grind, qualified and unqualified alike (some of them where the nephews, or in any case admirers, of management). Stipulated, they came. Flat black wheels, trucks, rails, decks, grip tape, bright yellow millennial jumpsuits. None of it ironic.

The skateboards had arrived to be tested.

"Another day, another fifty cents," Piotr said, and got up.

"I guess we'd better start checking them in," Thomas grumbled, scanner in hand.

It was one of those days where Piotr had woken up worryingly chatty. Holding forth ebulliently on topics he usually played close to his tight-fitting brown vest. Most of it classified.

All in all the skateboards were easy to work with. Flat, matte black. Even in the sun's glare they were easy to look at, if difficult to see. Thomas' chief concern was that, indeed, they were so alien to his way of seeing things, the way they simply absorbed whatever light was thrown at them, that he wasn't sure they could ever assimilate.

That was where Geo came in.

A North American great horned owl, Geo was the lead contractor, also an avid skateboarder, and had, during his travels, picked up some of their lingo. He could communicate with the things, anticipating their desires as well as their ultimate end users' desires, and demanded only a cursory fee, well within the project's budget, for his contributions. Thomas suspected Geo was doing it out of *love*, the putz.

Piotr wasn't so sure.

"You guys are the opposite of gnarly," Geo was saying, his hopelessly dated INFLUENCER patch displayed unironically upon his left wing-shoulder, "You can't even nollie properly." They had to get their numbers up.

"FFFFFFF..." one of the decks said, spinning its tiny black wheels. This batch of black skateboards could hardly speak owing to an acute lack of onboard audio. What the skateboard had been trying to express was that the term "gnarly" embodied two distinct, contradictory definitions. It was a contronym.

"I know," Geo said.

It was going to be a long session.

▦ Down the silo, nobody really understood what was happening. Didn't even know they were siloed. Each official's subjective experience was inescapably mediated by convention, solidified by tradition, congealed into *de facto* law through the nominal style in which they carried out their work day. Nobody had time to question minor irregularities, or to indulge in long-term thinking. This predictably affected the success rate of self-preservation. Life here was brief, if rarely properly violent.

The senators were idiots.

Thomas had considered running for office, but was reminded at intervals of his longstanding prohibition against accumulating personal power. He found himself jolted rudely by the clownish machinations of these elected officials, down the hole. Working closely such a buffoonish collection of small-minded crooks kept him honest.

Piotr climbed the step ladder and adjusted a dilapidated sign above the entrance of the senate chamber. "Let The Stress Begin," it read.

Legislating *was* stressful, Thomas knew. He couldn't begin to imagine the pressure these brave men and women must be under, what with carrying out their duties during this present emergency, whatever it was, and simply tolerating each other, day in, day out.

"Stress is right," he heard one of them complain as they passed under Piotr's sign.

A freshman.

Ralph lay spread eagle on the floor of the senate chamber. Unconscious. Nude.

"See if his dick's cold," Piotr commanded.

Thomas touched the tip of his data glove to the bell-end of Ralph's penis. It was cold. Instantly, his visor lit up with sensor data.

"It's like I always say," Piotr continued, "Where there's smoke, there's a phenomenon that induces the perception of smoke." Still worryingly chatty.

"Too true," Thomas agreed, scanning on all wavelengths for a source of heat. But there was no there, there.

Ralph's entire body was cold.

Why was Ralph here, now? Why, after all these years, had he tracked them down, seemingly at the direction of the enemy?

Piotr had clammed up after that second day of questioning. Thomas figured the chatterbox routine had taken its toll and his partner would need some downtime to recharge his batteries. This left Thomas to his own devices, which were, conspicuously, still fully operational. He'd have to wing it.

It had been many years since any of them had seen Ralph. For all they knew he could have gone into politics, might even have already been here, on Mars, under a different name and job title. Thomas had always assumed Ralph was dead.

The evidence to the contrary was damning. First of all, Ralph's approach to the silo had been all wrong. Anyone with his background should have realized the peripheral awareness would detect him. Or even the RAGNAROK, for fuck's sake. But not Ralph. And here he was wearing the uniform of a hostile force. Something about this scenario was suspicious, all right.

Thomas paused the investigation. It was time for lunch.

▦ For Ralph, the experience had been far from routine. First, the client had sent him into the field without providing proper targeting data. He'd spent the entire first morning getting himself oriented—that is to say, getting himself pointed in the right direction relative to the silo, wherever that ended up being located. Then there had been the hike across the desert. His gear had gotten clogged with sand. And he hadn't even been told he'd be working underground. None of it was fair.

"Well, the eggheads swear that the sun isn't burning coal," he heard Thomas saying.

"Accurate," he heard Piotr reply. Technically, he was right.

These guys hadn't changed a bit.

But hey, wait a minute. What were *they* doing out here? *This* hadn't been mentioned in the brief, either.

Naturally, Ralph found himself unprepared. Now he guessed he'd have plenty of time to adjust. Gradually, the impromptu reunion of old schoolmates extended into weeks, and then months of intense questioning, deep in the silo.

Old hands at the question and answer game, they certainly had a lot to catch up on. But lately Ralph was starting to question the questioning itself. He'd met a new transfer named Jerrymander who was steadily filling his head with all sorts of confusing ideas. For one thing, why had a facility such as this been erected on *Mars,* of all places? Jerrymander seemed to know a little bit about everything, which made him especially irresistible to a *self-confessed idiot* like Ralph. But, *wait.* Somehow Jerrymander had still managed to find himself confined *here,* sharing a six-by-six cell with, well, a self-confessed idiot like Ralph. It was perplexing.

And of course there were additional questions. Why was everyone pretending that Super-Sonic was a medical doctor? Wasn't that illegal? Baffled, he bowed his head to pray.

Mornings he usually spent working on the fundamentals. Who *was* he, and how did he know for sure? How did he *know* that he knew? Was identity itself a source of friction detrimental to the economy? This particular bit he usually sailed through with little difficulty. It was easy: he was Ralph. What more was there to say?

But on and on the workout would grind, and the nagging voice in his head continued to whisper: *Could that ever be enough?*

Shut up, he would hiss at himself, rhythmically, between reps.

"Field trip around the sun," Piotr said, jerking his thumb over his shoulder toward the triangular pink spacecraft who was also his mother.

"He means that literally," Thomas muttered out of the corner of his mouth.

Ralph got himself up.

Thomas placed a gloved hand on Ralph's shoulder, pulled hard. Suddenly finding his legs swept out from under him, Ralph had no choice but to collapse involuntarily into the dust.

"Not so fast, dipshit. *You'll* never leave this place alive."

everythings_gone_green

I've had dreams   of us cuddling on the planet Mars
— Prince, *Space*

░░ Evident along the pathway were the occasional clear-
ings, open spaces relatively lacking in tree cover (and thus, in
near-field surveillance). The lag could be exploited in various ways. Bear decided to test the limits of exploitation.

Crossing the pasture would draw the attention of certain locals bent on collecting a finder's fee. Of course, they
would never tell his parents. He paid them and left.

He could still feel the breeze on his neck. He could still
hear the trees whispering behind his back even as he decided
to remain silent about his role in tonight's events. There
would be no accounting for his efforts, which he hoped
would remain forever obscured.

He walked home and slipped quietly into his room. No
messages, which was fine. Half asleep, bear lay down on his
bed and covered his face with his blanket.

Stupid bear.

Get out of bed.

It was always the same field he had to cross in order to get back home. Bear would leave and come back. One thing he could always count on was the sinking feeling he'd get whenever he was stopped for conversation. Locals.

Bear never chatted for long. He would nod, grunt, and then make his excuses. Some of them would get the message. Others he would have to eat.

He hoarded all the best bits in his den. A collector's collector. He was aware that the extent and condition of his massive collection would vex his contemporaries. Of course, he didn't broadcast his good fortune. It was nearly winter.

And he was once again trying to record. The tape machine was being finicky in its usual way. It was true he had slacked off on maintenance, but the damned thing was hard to work with even on a good day. No, no more degaussing. He tried one last take and then he put his equipment away. Later for this.

The field and his den sometimes seemed like the whole world. These two miserable tracts.

Bear's mind wandered.

The dialectic of field and den strained under the immense weight of bear's concentration. One no longer seemed entirely distinct from the other. His interests had become global. As he searched the firmament for the borderlands he knew must exist, he encountered diverse locals, new locales, but no clearly defined borders. Some of them he knew and remembered, some vexed him with unfamiliar language and customs.

Bear knew all the citizens of this binary world were capable of more, so much more.

It was simply a matter of uncovering their boundaries, then expanding their awareness slowly to move beyond them. Bear felt instinctively that he was ready. The others he wasn't so sure about.

Carefully, he began to sketch a map.

But it was all coming out in the wrong colors. Bear across the meadow, bear just as he was. He could feel the pressure building behind his gleaming black eyes. He used his words. This was how it worked. But after a while the words were no longer enough.

"Tell me," said bear, "What will I think of next?"

Pinpricks in his spine.

Time to go home.

Bear was concerned there was no way he would hear the chime when it was time for him to wake up. He lit a candle and at the bottom he placed a favor that would be set off by the flame. It was the best he could do.

Out in the field he could hear the nightly cacophony. They weren't bugs, really. Depending on how you understood the word. It was difficult to describe the sound. Anyway, no one was paying him to listen.

Bear could remember liking this time of year. It was something he held onto, especially on those nights when he wasn't feeling well. Down in his back, like most other nights on most other worlds. Bear wondered if this was normal. Is this how it was for the other bears?

Were there other bears?

It was cold.

Bear kept his blanket over his face. He went over the story in his head but he could never quite remember the order of things as he wanted to remember them. It was a real challenge to stay awake, especially when he set his mind to it.

Bear slept.

In his dream he saw the things he had tried to explain, with all of it seeming to make sense to the others who were present, ever listening. It never quite worked out that way in the waking world. Everyone was always so confused. That was not to say that bear preferred being asleep. He only wanted to translate aspects of his experience into waking life. A way to communicate what he had seen and felt.

There was no one for bear to tell this to.

What would he think of next?

Abandoning such questions, he would get out of bed and walk in the field.

The locals had learned to leave him alone. They knew by now that he was broke. You can't bleed a turnip, as his grandmother used to say. Bear was no turnip, but he thought he understood what she meant.

He heard his chime. Bear wasn't sure which day it was anymore. In practice it probably didn't matter. It was time to get up.

He set out across the field and quickly rediscovered the spot where he had left off the day before. Continued.

The prospect of reaching the other side of the field, without being interrupted, without being stopped for the toll, for small talk, or for some other form of tribute, was something he felt he still believed in, however remote the possibility might seem to a more reasonable mind. Bear allowed his own mind to wander where it might, sometimes venturing to unlikely places. It was how he stayed awake. It was how he stayed sane.

His neighbor wanted to know how long he'd be away.

Stay out of my room, said bear. He was serious, and he growled to prove it. His neighbor laughed.

Bear would remember to take an inventory of his belongings when at last he returned from the field.

▦ The green of the field had worn a line around bear's waist, cresting just below his navel where he leaned into its curve as he ran. The sensation was not altogether unpleasant, but bear didn't allow himself the distraction. The grass flowed smoothly around him, drawing tight in his wake, a soft curtain of green closing on an empty stage.

Oh, no.

He'd overtaken the transition.

Failure in this, his own field, would not go unnoticed. Was there any point in trying to explain? Bear would continue to make mistakes. Anyway, he knew what he had found even if the locals couldn't be made to understand. He folded his discovery in half and tucked it under his arm. The firmament was still cooling, its pages might still singe. Bear gripped the fabric with intent as he retreated into the woods. Now he would wait, and listen.

Beyond today's failure loomed certain possibilities. Bear could feel it in his fur. Intrinsic to the locals' tolerance of his presence was the assumption of a shared frame of reference, or at least, a unified conception of the ground rules by which they all agreed to coexist. Bear was now prepared to discard such trappings as delusional. His discovery transcended the treachery of images, the befuddlement of emptiness. He understood, at long last, that language is theft.

The field beckoned.

Bear was hungry.

From one side to the other, alternating endlessly, cycling mechanically, bear ran, and he knew that he ran. The awareness cresting in him, the familiar sense of self welling up, lubricating the machinery of his confusion.

It was enough.

It was a live birth. Bear descended into the world on tired paws. His way out of this mess. He assumed,

His new parents quickly disabused him of the notion. Not that it was strictly their fault. The shared construct prevented them deviating to any significant extent. How it was designed. Yes, it was a setup.

Bear was hungry.

Here, someone fed him. They taught him what they knew. Maybe that was the problem. Bear always felt there was something missing, but he couldn't quite put his finger (paw?) on it. His memory of the field was fading.

On bear's ninth birthday he awoke from the dream. The locals had been trying to tell him something, all along. *He would have to give it all back.* But he didn't know what that was supposed to mean. It was frustrating.

As a young man bear learnt many of the things his parents would never know. Some of the things he had simply forgotten from before. Some of them were unknown even to the locals. At times he felt that he could almost remember the breeze, in the grass...

Before he knew it it was once again time for him to return to the field. Somehow, deep down, he'd known it all along.

Everything went green.

the_end

A moth ate words. That seemed to me a curious happening, when I heard about that wonder, that the worm, a thief in the darkness, swallowed a certain man's song, a glory-fast speech and its strong foundation. The stealing guest was not at all the wiser for that, for those words which he swallowed.

— Exeter Book Riddle 47

▦ New York, 2020.

Tom tracked the moth's progress with uncharacteristic interest as the insect traced a diagonal path across the inside of his visor. Annoyingly, it was interfering with his vision. He batted his eyelashes, but the tiny moth stubbornly remained affixed to he underside of the handsfree display. There was nothing left to say. He was going to have to kill the damned thing.

Tom ripped the visor from his face and flung it hard across the room, where presently it skidded to a dull stop. Now fully blind, he realized with a start that he could no longer see to kill *anything*. His situation would appear to have degraded. In fact, it had both degraded and improved.

He no longer had to contend with the moth fucking up his display. On the other hand, he could no longer see, at all. The balance of the Force.

Tom pressed the button on his belt that called for his secretary.

Too much of his time lately had been spent in this fashion. Grasping at fantasies, wallowing in confusion. Tom longed for the smell of battle. It had been... too long. Years prior he had donated all his weapons to the children's mission. It seemed like such a long time ago, now.

"That's because it was," Piro said, responding to Tom's unspoken lament.

Tom ignored him.

▦ Tom regarded his newly silvered hair in the mirror. He looked tired. True, there were problems down at the office. The latest batch of cocaine had all turned black. There was an opportunity for a joke, here, but wisely, Tom demurred. He was doing that a lot lately—demurring. Was it an artifact of his increasing weariness?

It was not like him to stand around and reflect. But, well, here he was, in front of the mirror. And he was just so damned pretty.

Tom touched his fingers to his lips and then he touched them to the mirror. Planting a little kiss, just like the old days. "Too fine," he said, sadly. And he was.

Sad, that is.

The pink triangle badge on his polo shirt illuminated dimly. It was time for his conference call. He finished up at the sink and made his way over to the neutral backdrop strung up behind his prop desk. Straightened his visor and joined the call.

There they were. The whole team was there. Yep, perfect attendance. In reality it was more of the same. He hated to micromanage, but he couldn't help noticing the violations.

His employees were just so stupid. Stupid enough to work for him, anyway, which in his book entitled them to his unending abuse. More of which would always be forthcoming.

Nearly thirty years had passed since he'd taken over the A.C.T.R.O.N. team, sans Piro. In all that time there hand't been any firings or new hires. Everyone here was a veteran player—a classic character, long established with the fanbase—so they'd all been around the block together more than a few times. They all knew what to say, how to stand. They all knew the score.

Knowing this, he found it impossible to respect any of them.

▦ Of course, the silver in his hair was a fake. It had been many years since he'd aged. If it were up to him he'd skip the pantomime, ludicrous as it was, but his investors expected a certain bogus *gravitas,* the more blatantly bogus the better. These days, he dressed like a high school basketball coach working weekends at a car dealership.

Grisham's Formula. He smeared the commercial paste across his forehead and kneaded it into his scalp. Firmly, so there could be no escape. They'd think of him as just another bad dad. This stuff really worked.

For the conference calls it probably didn't matter. Nobody he'd be speaking to cared how he looked or sounded. But for the sake of his brand he kept himself on model. You never knew who might be monitoring remotely. And he found it easier to keep track of himself this way.

Now, where was he?

Thirty-six employees were being let go. The annual surplus. It was time to make the announcement.

▦ The firings went about as well as could be expected, under the circumstances. Nobody wanted to be laid off, which was understandable. But the readymade disloyalty came as a surprise to Tom. After three decades they all turned on him instantly.

Dimension Man: "I just don't see why we're cutting headcount in a record profit year."

Sonic Boom: "We've been speculating about this all day, and boy are my arms tired."

Eva: "I can't believe I'm even still sitting here."

Super Sonic: [Glancing at Eva, opening a new line of subtext] "Let's go."

Eva and Super Sonic exit.

Raven: "Ha ha. All this because the coke turned black? White people are hilarious."

No. *That* wasn't it.

He hadn't fired anyone that day. What was he *thinking?* He was confusing *today* with that *other* time, in that *other* place.

Tom slapped himself.

Snap out of it, idiot.

He tried again.

The firings went about as well as could be expected considering no one was getting fired. Nobody said anything rash. Nobody said anything, at all. He was heartened by the team's unanimous expression of support for his difficult decision. For the first time in a long time he felt like a real leader.

Dimension Man: "I figure, they're not going to cut headcount in a record profit year."

Sonic Boom: "The suits are picking up the bill!"

Eva: "Oh my God, I was sure we were all getting fired."

Super Sonic: [Snoring] [But faking it]

Raven: "Ha ha. So what do we do with all this black coke?"

That was more like it.

▦ The moth had made good its escape with auspicious timing. Stopped eating the words out from under the author. Had it ever really been there? Good moth.

Tom was a good boss.

He'd kept them all working in the Chrysler Building Classic while the New Chrysler Building was growing up, supplanting the original building's cultural status. (Seventy-seven stories weren't what they used to be.) Some of his employees had grumbled, but he figured eventually the vintage chronolocation would come back into style, vindicating his decision and making it seem as if he had known what he was doing all along.

They were all still waiting.

Which kept the rents low.

▦ New York, 1987.

Thomas sat and fiddled with his pocket radio.

Either *sound* had changed, or he had. Nothing sounded the same. In point of fact, he didn't even recognize what he was hearing. He spun the dial up and down the spectrum, confused. So far, 1987 was diminishing returns.

"Tom, you're senile." Piro laid a hand on his shoulder. The gesture had always annoyed him.

"You're too familiar," Tom said, and shrugged his hand away, righteously rejecting this invasion of his personal space. Didn't care if Piro *was* his brother. He hadn't given consent, so, keep your fucking hands to yourself.

Contrary to expectation, plugging in the balanced cable had *reduced* apparent bass response. Subjectively. Another hundred bucks down the drain. Thomas didn't really understand what he was doing, but this didn't make any sense. He diddled again with the connectors, to no effect.

"I *hate* music," he said, to no one.

"Oh, it's not *all* that bad," sighed the Chrysler Building Classic.

Thomas muted his visor.

▦ New York, 2020.

It was time to dye his hair again.

Tom kneaded the Grisham's Formula into his scalp and waited for it to take effect. The inevitable sales boost would hit like a four day weekend. Ah, here it came now.

Was this stuff affecting him?

Could *anything* affect him?

Just being born had been traumatic enough. But nowadays he had to contend with efficiency stats, human resources protocols, public relations snafus, labor boards, local agreements, office politics, quarterly budgets, and the fact that this hair dye recalcitrantly refused to turn his hair completely silver. He looked like a young man wearing an old man costume. But in a bad way. Everything he did to try and accentuate his apparent age only made him look more and more like a little boy wearing his father's clothes.

He wasn't going deaf, he thought. If anything, his superpowers had intensified with age. He was stronger. He was faster. And he was pretty sure his hearing had actually improved. Therefore, he could only conclude that *sound itself* had degraded. Hadn't he been saying that all along?

Crushed the pocket radio (where had *that* thing come from?) in his super-powered fist, scattering electronic dust across his low pile carpet.

His reverie was disrupted by yet another call from Piro.

Which was curious, since Piro had been dead for thirty years.

The concept of this stable inner core is ancient and tenacious, but it is an illusion.

— attributed

▦ Even after he crushed it in his fist the thing still kept working. So he shut it off. Still, it kept playing.

Nuts.

They had all died.

As much as Tom could now remember, he was aware that there was still much more he had forgotten. Whole people, entire eras. The continuity was by now completely muddled. Hardly acknowledged by the creative staff. And he didn't even have an editor.

Piro was gone, of that much he was certain. But his memory of the pirate persisted. Tom found that it helped to keep things straight if he pretended to have conversations with his dead brother. He could write down their dialogue, it even continued as he slept. In fact, he found that he couldn't turn it off.

Begrudgingly, Tom took dictation of the new stories. He didn't really sleep at night. His coworkers were useless idiots. No speakers produced enough bass. No one was really believing his silver hair, except for the people who would agree reflexively with anything he said, and their opinions didn't count.

His back hurt.

Shut up.

▦ Space, 2047.

Piro was still dead.

Nowadays, Tom found himself marooned in an isolation cell of his own design. Solitary confinement, shipping himself back to DET-86 aboard a miniaturized RAGNAROK shuttle he'd chiseled off from the main ship while she wasn't looking. He'd booked the flight himself, bereft beyond belief at his current status, re: dead relatives. Somehow, this would make it all better.

What did he imagine was waiting for him at the other end of his journey?

Unknown.

He pressed a button on his cell door that opened his tiny observation window. Snaked his arm through the hole, fishing for the exterior door handle.

Let himself out.

The craft was small. Minimal library. No auxiliary inputs. No galley. He rummaged under the seats for snacks, found his stash.

It was going to be a long trip. The shuttle refused to activate his visor, and so he remained effectively blind. But this couldn't stop him from thinking about the past. There was no one around to interrupt him.

His mind wandered back, to the late 1980s...

▦ This time there would be no reprieve. Tom closed his eyes. And then he opened them again. But he was still there, aboard the ship. Still thinking about [redacted].

He was pretty sure.

Flashed through the visible spectrum. Must be dark by now, but it was hard to tell, what with the dead visor and all. (Also, space.) He'd lost the little wrench he used to remove the now useless strip of plastic from his face. Nothing to be done, then, until the ship docked at DET–86.

Mars.

Yes, it was going to be a long trip. He'd purposely locked the ship into a reduced velocity transit. Voice commands disabled. Without his visor there would be no way to alter course. It figured. It was very much like himself to change his mind only after it was too late for him to do anything about it.

Space, at this speed, was pretty boring. Forward in time, one pre-defined unit of measurement after another. It was not at all apparent from riding in the cabin that he was even advancing toward his objective, whatever that might be.

Each thought progressed a half-step beyond the last, never quite arriving at its target, like some kind of dipshit's arrow, forever transiting a fraction of the measurable frontier. He was boring himself speechless. It was a dead-end sentence.

[...]

It couldn't have been *this* bad, back when he was in charge.

⠿ "I'm an idiot," Tom said, aloud.

There was no argument from the crew, who were in any case not aboard the ship, and therefore hadn't heard his remark. Likewise, they would have had no way to respond, even if some perfunctory audio feed had been provided to them, back on Earth. Convenient.

Tom slumped in his captain's chair, still moping about his predicament. He opened another bag of chips. The pattern had become apparent even to himself. He watched himself eat the chips and then he watched himself wipe his hands across the front of his shirt.

What was he doing?

Well, there was no one to ask.

His eyes drew to a slit beneath his ruined visor.

Waitaminute.

It was at this precise moment that Tom finally recalled his childhood. The whole strange shape of it, a smearing, quicksilver ellipsoid, entering and exiting his mind like a tadpole shooting across a pond. Or, yes, like a bullet through his brain.

Bang.

And then, nothing. As quickly as it had arrived, the awareness evaporated into nothingness. No ripple, no impression was left behind in the fizzle of Tom's conscious awareness. His revelation was just as quickly forgotten, proving once and for all that a thing seen can most certainly be unseen.

Unaware of the momentary disturbance, Tom returned automatically to his chips.

Continued the mission.

▦ Tom hummed along with the low whine in the cabin and drummed his gloved fingers absentmindedly on his console. At some point he became aware of a counterrhythm interpolating his performance. It seemed he had a visitor.

Yooouuu refuse to talk, but you think like mad

A K.A.R.L. unit slowly whirred to life, seemingly annoyed at the effrontery of his own existence. The animatronic musician could never just be satisfied with the status of his own career. He killed the canned soundtrack and studied his new master with arch incredulity.

"What are you doing to yourself?" he finally asked, quoting his own lyrics to the ridiculous figure splayed before him on the captain's chair.

Tom hadn't known a K.A.R.L. had been installed in his shuttle. It figured, though. Simulated companionship, a perfunctory dose of what ailed him. Well, this could indeed be just what the doctor ordered. A little bump, if you will.

"The coke's all turned black," K.A.R.L. complained. "No criticism of you, mind, but obviously I can't work under these conditions. What am I supposed to do? Mark up my face?"

So, no.

"I don't really care *what* you do, but you're going to do it off this ship," Tom said, softly, not really feeling the weight of his words. He reached for the assisted egress but mistakenly pulled the wrong lever. The cabin's ambient tranquility was once again flattened by K.A.R.L.'s brickwalled (courtesy of Tony Visconti) soundtrack as the erstwhile synthetic performer involuntarily sprung back into action.

And even your eyes are new

Tom's visor steamed over. Fingers in his ears, he couldn't pull any more levers.

K.A.R.L.'s assembly clicked, popped, and whirred as he worked through the remainder of his pre-recorded program. Tom regarded the choreography as dated, corny. With his routine finally completed, K.A.R.L. relaxed his stance and resumed his original complaint as if there had been no inter-ruption.

"Just can't score any satisfaction," he said.

Tom was sympathetic, if ultimately unable to help. *All* of the coke had turned black. This, at least, was true.

"Everybody's had a rough year."

Both entities reclined and contemplated the silence of space.

▦ The route between Earth and Mars was the same one Tom had traveled a million times during his youth. Going to work with Dad. Coming home with Dad. Going to work with Piro. Etcetera. He reviewed the highlights with K.A.R.L.

"Sometimes when I'm bored, I just *count,*" Tom said. "It's a pretty long trip, so, sometimes I get up to a pretty high number. I can usually guess pretty well how far we've traveled based on how far I've progressed up the number line."

K.A.R.L. stared straight through him. He didn't get this at all.

"I guess I just don't have the imagination," K.A.R.L. finally said. "I've never been good with numbers."

"Hm," Tom allowed. "Anyway, during the war, Dad wouldn't let me *talk* during the trip, so I had to come up with my own entertainment. Counting seemed fun, for a while at least."

Crickets.

Tom wasn't sure if K.A.R.L. had fallen asleep, or what. He waited several minutes, then nudged the mechanical entity, who presently started back to life.

"Uh huh, yes, do go on."

Tom gave him a look.

"You could say I taught myself," Tom continued.

"Right, right," K.A.R.L. said.

It was a long interview.

▓▓ Silence reclaimed the cabin.

K.A.R.L. had finally run down. Fulfilling the guarantee of his pre-recorded program, he sagged gently into deep sleep mode. Tom climbed back into his isolation cell and engaged the locks. With both observation windows open, he could reach through on both sides and *just* touch either inner wall of the cabin, wearing his cell like a t-shirt. It transpired that the scope of his self-imposed imprisonment was limited only by his strength of will, tempered by the fixed size of his spacecraft.

He sighed.

Back and forth. How many times in his life had he made this trip? When would he ever decide where he wanted to be?

Indeed, Tom.

He tried to whistle to himself, but in the dry air of the cabin nothing came out. In addition to this, his lips were getting chapped.

Presently, K.A.R.L. resumed.

"I *hate* Indiana," he said.

Tom ignored the *non sequitur.* Indiana—its existence—whether or not it sucked, had never figured significantly in his plans. If not for Woody on CHEERS, he would never have even heard of the place.

"So what," Tom said. "Pass the chips."

▓ Days, perhaps weeks later, nothing much had changed. Every day Tom carried out his same dreary routine with the same solemn competence.

K.A.R.L., for his part, had broken down. Entirely.

Reader, he was out of warranty. But, being in space, there was nothing Tom could do but complain. He couldn't ship him back to wherever he'd come from. Couldn't even throw him away.

"What a piece of junk."

He kicked the defective equipment, scoffed. K.A.R.L. just sat there and took it. Tom considered it endemic to mechanical life forms, machines, accepting any amount of abuse from a recognized authority figure. They had no capacity for rebellion. No innate urge to creative mischief. He just couldn't relate.

Pause for firmware update.

At length Tom's download completed and the shuttle resumed its journey.

Tom counted to one hundred, two hundred, three hundred, and beyond. By the time he finally finished, he had lost his place.

So, he started over.

One thought continued to nag at him: Who was this voice counting in his head?

▦ Things were moving slowly. More slowly now than usual. There was space, and then there was the trip between Earth and Mars. There weren't even any other vehicles out here to clog up his route. So why, then, the delay? Tom wasn't normally one for road rage, but this was getting out of hand.

He decided to read a book.

(Wait for it.)

From the pile at his feet he pulled a biographical treatment of his father, prepared decades before by an Agency historian. He'd asked for it at the last minute before setting off on his journey. Now he figured he'd have time to read the whole thing.

Right off the bat he found something to complain about.

First, they had spelled his family name wrong.

▓ "Is there any part of you that isn't just a reaction to some perceived slight?" K.A.R.L. abruptly spun back to life, without warning. Wit intact, his tart opening lines always cheered Tom up.

"No," Tom said, and switched him back off again. K.A.R.L.'s wit was actually wearing a bit thin.

He was right, though. Tom's visor was still down. He couldn't *really* read the biography of his father, and so there was really nothing in there (so far as he knew) to be angry about. He'd invented the detail about the spelling of his family name just to amuse himself. He had no way of knowing, in fact, that he had even picked up the right book.

So, reading was no good. But still Tom was jittery. What did he expect to happen next? Why did he keep asking himself these stupid questions? Why did the robot keep reading his mind?

The cabin was so damned hot he was leaving an outline on the pilot's seat.

▦ And now he was being tailgated.

Out here, on this route, it was rare. But the sensors didn't (so far as he knew) lie. Another spacecraft had come up just behind him, external effects flaring/ Suspiciously close, aggressively flashing its lights.

It was hailing him.

He made the effort to respond.

"TAB2, responding to suspicious tailgater," he sighed into his sleeve mic.

"Tom. Glad I caught up with you out here," said an unfamiliar voice. "I wanted to be the first to tell you the news."

Grant Morrison's great-great-grandson was taking over as writer on Disney's EVEN NEWER X-MEN. History repeating itself, Tom knew that he had better get in on the ground floor, had better get his hands on those issues, even if it meant once again setting foot inside a comic shop.

He would have to figure out how to turn this shuttle around.

▦ New York, 2020.

Finally back at his desk, Tom removed his visor and rubbed his ruined eyes. Everything was safely in its place: the framed picture of his family, the lucite block containing a laser etching of a Lockheed Martin F–35A (a paperweight, get it?), the news clippings, the magazine photos of the original A.C.T.R.O.N. team he still kept pinned to the wall. He sipped his coffee and pressed the button that called his secretary.

"Eva, could you come in here, please."

Chrysler Building Classic systems must have been on the fritz. Several minutes elapsed, and finally Tom wasn't sure if his secretary had got the message. Just as he was about to try again, the speaker on his desk squawked to life.

"I'm not your secretary," she finally said. And it was true. Instead, she was his wife. "What do you want?"

"Have the comics been delivered yet?" he asked, sounding rather more desperate than he had intended.

She had no idea. Why was he asking *her?*

"Oh. Well, okay. Sorry to bother you."

It was Wenesday. The comics *should* have been delivered by now, but Eva didn't care about that kind of thing, so it had probably slipped her mind.

He sunk back into his chair. Was he really going to have to walk all the way down to the comic shop by himself?

Enter Piro, the pirate.

"Why don't you just download them?" he said.

"Down*what?*" Tom asked, forever perplexed. Head of an interstellar drug empire for nearly three decades, he hadn't yet found out about comics piracy.

But there would be no reply to his very many questions.

Piro was really dead.

No. That wasn't right, either.

Piro hadn't been dead when he'd figured out how to torrent comics. It had been Piro who had helped him with his router settings.

What was happening to his memory?

He kept on rubbing his eyes. The bridge of his nose was sore, screaming from the frame of his visor. At some point he realized his visor had in fact gone missing. Gone, but now he could *see*. And the bridge of his nose still hurt. How could this be?

Sharp rapping at his cell window and the little access door slid open. It was his lunch. A small tray breached the tiny slot, like a tongue extending from a panther's mouth. He accepted it readily.

Tom hated the freeze-dried mashed potatoes, hated the cardboard carrots, but the frozen peas were okay. He skipped the rest and downed his beverage in a single gulp.

That's when he noticed the note from his dad.

Kid, don't crack on me now. Your government has invested significant tax-payer dollars in your future. Don't throw away our hard work based on some silly misunderstanding. Let's keep politics out of it, okay? Hell, isn't that what you signed up for? In any case, don't embarrass me. I'm only going to tell you this once: Do your job.

Love,

Dad

▦ A message from *whom?*

It was enough to put him off his peas. Something wasn't right. Aside from the string of disconnected clichés, the half-hearted tax protest, and the obsession with his own social standing, the handwriting was definitely not his father's. And, much like Piro, his father was long dead.

When had this been written? And for whom?

Tom tapped his tray absentmindedly. He heard a soft click as it came unlatched. He removed the now dangling cover to reveal a hidden compartment, surprisingly deep (deeper on the inside, in fact, than should have been possible, given the size of the tray), which contained a secondary payload.

An 8" x 10" glossy photograph of a Timex Sinclair 1000, complete with 16 KB RAM pack. Something inside of him shifted, responding to the apparent visual trigger.

Tom touched his visor, connecting the now corporeal device to a panel on his cell door with a touch of his free hand.

The lights went out.

His cell door opened.

SL fled.

no_memory

You blame yourself for   what you   can't ignore
— The Smashing Pumpkins, *Zero*

NO VISOR

Two hundred years later, commence perpetual dusk.

Cue Kraftwerk. Or, just write your own.

K.A.R.R. squinted at the flat expanse, incredulous at the monotonous flatness of that same, boring horizon. In his head he repeated a snatch of unrelated music, culminating in the fragmented lyric: "orgasmic waste for the seven senses." Indeed, he thought. Already he was repeating himself.

He blinked out an alternate musical sequence to trigger his memory settings. Scrolling through the options, he happened upon an unfinished simulacrum and resumed authoring the clip. It was a pitch from back in middle school for a vintage SNL skit: Chris Farley as the Incredible Hulk. The transformation sequence from the 1970s show, with Farley in civilian clothes roiding out into Farley as the Hulk. Only, Farley wasn't ragequitting his western style snap shirt and denims slacks, he was simply yawning. Shirt rips. Pants rip.

Cut to a shot of his eyes, bloodshot from lack of sleep. Face going slack—not angry, but *exhausted.* Humorous because Farley was famously, morbidly obese. End skit.

K.A.R.R. saved his progress, kicked off a test render, and then took a long pull from his bubble pipe.

Nobody out here at this time of night, thank god who didn't exist.

K.I.T.T. raced across the desert floor every bit as fast as his gleaming dark vehicle could take him, tracking mere inches above the rapidly cooling sand. Yes, he was wasting fuel, but K.A.R.R. was out here, somewhere. Waiting. It was already (still?) dusk. Calories trickled out of his exhaust in the form of sound. Truth be told, it was taking a toll on his ears, though he wouldn't become aware of the fact until several decades hence.

Prodigious clouds of dust obscured his approach. If not for the interminable *WUPPA   WUPPA   WUPPA* of K.I.T.T.'s propulsion system, K.A.R.R. might never have become aware that he was no longer alone. As it was, K.A.R.R. had stopped paying attention, enjoying his solitude, and he was startled anew whenever K.I.T.T. got close enough to kick rocks into his field of vision.

K.I.T.T. reduced window opacity and motioned for K.A.R.R. to get in.

These two would not quarrel today.

Streaking towards home, smearing red sand in their wake, they began to talk.

"I wasn't really finished, you know."

"Bonnie doesn't care."

K.A.R.R. accepted the obvious because it was true. Bonnie probably would have preferred it if he wasn't out here at all, so far from town center. But there were worse things he could have been doing with his time. Mostly, Bonnie left him alone to work through his simulacra.

"What happened to your hair?"

There was no real reason why K.A.R.R. needed to come home for dinner. He could just as easily have packed a lunch. But sometimes these little interruptions relieved the pressures that bore down on him so oppressively. It gave him a chance to regroup before re-attaching to whatever project currently occupied his agenda. In this example, Chris Farley could wait.

"I got rid of it, okay?"

K.A.R.R.'s bubble pipe had run out of bubbles. He tapped the cylinder, forlorn at the sudden realization he'd forgotten to pack extra mixture. So here was a reason to stop by home, after all.

"It's your turn to be the bad guy," K.I.T.T. said at once, smiling to himself in the rear-view mirror.

No. K.A.R.R. was not going to quarrel, today.

K.A.R.R. clocked in at home and sat himself down for a quick dinner. Per company police, he had only twenty-six minutes to clean his plate and police his dishes. Bonnie ran a disciplined operation, and she hadn't authorized overtime.

Next would be town center. If you could call it that. K.A.R.R. knew it was only a matter of time before the economy would pick up again, but a body marooned in these parts could be forgiven their doubts. Most of these businesses had been boarded over for years. Decades.

Ruins of the silo lay just beyond the town. Once, it had featured as the center of activity in the settlement. Now, most residents acted as if it didn't exist, if they remembered it at all. K.A.R.R. thought this was interesting. The place had obviously had something to do with the military. Information about it was scarce. He passed by the ruins on his way back to the desert. This time, without his visor.

DATABASE ANIMALS

It was the only time K.A.R.R. had ever fallen asleep out in the desert. He was busy cataloguing his failures, vis–à–vis K.I.T.T., when it happened. Started awake just before he hit the ground. He had come to just as he was falling.

Dusk.

So, the last time he had bothered, K.I.T.T. had insisted upon pushing even more details lifted from unrelated media into their narrative. A partial list of his latest infatuations included: NASCAR, Namor the Sub–Mariner, and, for some reason, the Falklands War. Some of these would make it into issue three.

K.A.R.R. had rejected NASCAR out of hand, without really knowing what it was all about. He guessed that K.I.T.T.'s sources were probably not much better informed, TBQH. Besides, the material was anachronistic, class crass. He rolled over in the sand. Why was he even out here?

K.I.T.T.'s susceptibility to whatever half–baked novelty snagged his attention had proven a consistent annoyance. The resulting work he produced most often resembled whatever garbage was currently being talked about by the most insipid of K.I.T.T.'s friends. At the same time, K.I.T.T. was incredibly sensitive to criticism. He took disagreements over taste personally. Which was why K.A.R.R. was more relieved than surprised when K.I.T.T. inevitably quit the company.

If I am destroyed, so shall you be, he remembered thinking, contrary to his actual feelings, which were as usual reliably blank. Where had *that* come from?

K.A.R.R.'s eyes went blurry. Without his visor he was oblivious to quite a lot of detail. Luckily, the landscape consisted primarily of wall-to-wall, undifferentiated pink. Even the sky, at dusk, was more or less this same color. Stylistic conformity, a real timesaver. It freed up his attention for more important tasks. What use would he have had for the increased resolution, he wondered? The details would only have irritated him.

In these moments of relative sensory deprivation the shapes and whorls he usually tried to ignore would settle down and coalesce into a sort of *fabliaux,* spread before his mind's eye like a colorful arrangement of unslabbed comic books. K.A.R.R. considered his visor's interface to be a metaphor for this process, and not the other way around. But now, perhaps for the first time, he realized that he'd never heard anyone express it in quite the same way. It seemed that whichever direction he faced, he would find himself affixed to the same monotonously rotating landscape, which seemed immune to confessing its situatedness via the usual method of empirically reverse engineering his POV. Walk too far in any one direction, the motionless/revolving horizon seemed to suggest, and you'd overtake yourself from behind. That was the nature of this world he lived upon. Static, but devolving. Sinking, spinning.

He was dizzy.

Called Bonnie, who dispatched K.I.T.T. to come and pick him up.

There would be no delay.

BOUND COMICS

K.A.R.R.'s own interests were decidedly singleminded. Wherever he went, whatever he was supposed to be doing, he was always on the lookout for new comic books. Within this category (comic books) he discriminated freely, snatching up whatever looked interesting, but ignoring the material that didn't. He saw no contradiction in being particular. Since most of his planet was covered with sand, and there were few habitations to speak of, he enjoyed few opportunities to exercise this most ruthless, discerning razor blade of his taste. He'd turn up his nose at whatever he didn't like. (In truth, he usually ended up buying whatever he found.)

"We're just going to go over your numbers for August."

Bonnie on the line. She'd called and interrupted just as K.A.R.R. had been starting his work. He'd already been told not to charge time to these calls. How, then, to account for his undivided participation?

"Your efficiency is way off."

K.A.R.R. of course knew the reason for his discrepancy. Since his recent suspension for falsifying company records, he had been reporting his time accurately as a matter of course. How to break it to his boss that the reason she wouldn't be getting her bonus this month was because he was no longer protecting her from the consequences of her own decisions?

"What can I do to improve?" he asked, earnestly. He was good at this.

"I just feel like people are playing games with their numbers," she said, ignoring his question. "I just want you to know, now is not the time to be playing with your job."

She clicked off.

K.A.R.R. guessed he was now free to get to work.

The new release was coming along nicely, but it was not going to release itself. K.A.R.R. organized his notes and assembled something resembling an orderly accounting of all the changes made since the last release. Some of the commit messages were above his head, but that wouldn't significantly hinder him from sorting the list into general categories, alphabetized. Next he would proceed to the crux of his real contribution: selecting the correct cognitive tone, the precise, faintly audible pitch of the associated propaganda. How to set the whole thing vibrating such that it slotted into an auspicious trajectory (rather than being ground into corn meal between the massive, competing gravities of nearby thought constructions) while still remaining legible to the semi-disinterested reader.

Indeed, K.A.R.R.

He double-tapped the side of his visor, momentarily switching contexts. Fourteen issues were missing from his binding map, and he intended to somehow finish tracking them all down before his nap this afternoon.

Unbeknownst to him, the brief context switch had triggered an alarm that would be flagged for managerial review.

"This is an investigation meeting," Bonnie announced, peering through her ridiculously oversized visor at K.A.R.R., who returned her confused gaze through the slowly cycling *woosh* of his own tastefully fitted yellow frames.

"Woosh," K.A.R.R.'s visor said.

"No. More. Personal. Use. Of. Company. Visors." Bonnie tapped her leaf as she read each word. Sentence pronounced, she smiled conspiratorially to herself. She had made it through the whole thing without having to ask for help.

"Okay," K.A.R.R. lied, and waited for her to continue.

But that was it.

Investigation concluded.

Garthe had loaded up Goliath with comics. The militarized tractor trailer rig was overweight, hauling crates of floppies to be bound somewhere across state lines. Though how *he* was supposed tell where the state lines were, out here in the middle of all this pink, remained a god damned mystery. It didn't matter. Garthe did what he was told.

Black smoke belched from Goliath's twin smoke stacks. Garthe laughed, seemingly at nothing, the potent evil he usually radiated now focused tightly through his trim mustache and beard. What was his problem, anyway?

He didn't notice K.A.R.R. laying motionless in the sand until it was too late to slow down.

2D COLLISION DETECTION

Human minds as the medium for conflicts waged by lower life forms.

Flatlands (plural) intersecting, obstructing the path of the mordant ant-crusher. Possibly intersecting with yet other, geometrically opposed flatlands, somewhere along the way. Stipulated: a complex, multifaceted surface, gleaming on borrowed time.

The blocks were projected in "3D." Actually, flat paintings in light of imagined real life constructions. Call them panes.

Panels.

K.A.R.R. suddenly realized that his visor was just displaying comics.

He took the fucking thing off, looked at it, turned it around in his hands.

Put it back on.

Garthe slammed on the brakes but by now Goliath was ignoring manual input. If anything the rig seemed to be accelerating. Garthe wrinkled his nose and pushed air through his nostrils as Goliath barreled toward the inert figure laying motionless in the sand. Welp. He'd have to pretend this was somehow intentional. He wrinkled his eyebrows and gripped the steering wheel even more tightly than before.

Without warning, haptics kicked back in. Luckily Garthe had never stopped tugging on the steering wheel. Goliath swerved madly, nearly toppling over, and narrowly avoided flattening K.A.R.R. into a 2D desert doormat. The rig, however, had become perilously unstable along the way.

That was when Goliath collided with what appeared to be a huge rock.

Trailer capsized. Comics everywhere. This strange little fellow rolling around, rubbing the wings of his cloak against the comic book pages, like some kind of frolicking honey bee, oblivious to the danger. How had this been allowed to happen?

Garthe was beside himself. He'd spoiled the whole load. How was he going to explain this to his dad?

How indeed, Garthe?

Oh, and it hadn't been a rock that he'd hit, either. Garthe had run over another (smaller) vehicle. Not much left of it now, to be sure. A fine mess he'd gotten himself into.

He stroked his mustache pensively, trying to think of what he could do to salvage the load.

Nothing came to mind.

Comic books were falling from the sky, or rather, many, many pages thereof were twirling out everywhere, pinwheeling carelessly into the sand. K.A.R.R. grasped at them, fascinated. Most of these he recognized as key issues. It was too bad about the condition, but some of them could probably be ironed flat, sewn back together, or otherwise "minted." At least it was dry out here.

But by now it was too pink out to read. K.A.R.R. gathered

up the loose leaves as best he could before they floated away, tripping haphazardly into the unmarked desert. He had nothing to carry them in, so he ended up folding them into his cloak and heaving them over his shoulder, a big back–issue bindle, Martian Santa with his glistening black trash bag full of comic book crap.

Meanwhile, back at the scene of Garthe's final humiliation...

EMBITTERED B-MINUS COMPETITORS

Hi, it's me, SL.

In my capacity as author I have followed the ACTRON characters from my second grade year up until the present day, through photocopied comic books to literary novels to... whatever *this* is. Both the primary "living" protagonists—*Actron,* so named for an automotive diagnostic tool, and *Piro,* so called because he was a pirate— were in fact christened by my cousin, Brandon. We collaborated on a succession of half-baked (and usually unfinished) comic book series starting in 1986. ACTRON was the most successful, in the sense that I managed to complete drawing, scripting, reproducing, and distributing at least seven full issues during our initial burst of heedless enthusiasm. Brandon co-plotted (process: we traded off writing a paragraph–length description of every other comic book page), and, again, insisted upon inking, even though he otherwise did not draw.

As I say, Actron and Piro were and are alive. Fractally ever-present, verbally demanding, and definitely annoying. Writing about them is essentially transcribing an ongoing hallucination, although who is doing the hallucinating and who is ultimately being hallucinated eludes me to this day.

A few weeks ago I decided to stop.

Around 2003, I had resumed writing prose fiction. As an exercise, I strip mined reams of stories churned out since childhood. A chapter from my first novel written as an adult, 'Towards Mythologizing The Coming Resurgence Of Covert Warfare,' was lifted, wholesale and barely altered, from a novella I wrote for the Young Author's Conference in the fifth grade. None of its characters were alive, so to speak, but the *voice* stood up and walked all by itself. I built upon that skeleton, eventually piling hundreds of pages of semi-related nonsense atop the frankly inadequate scaffolding of my grade school writing. Rickety dwelling, no insurance, inhabit at your own risk. But it breathed, and, finally, walked all on its own.

In 2005, I decided to commemorate ACTRON's upcoming 20th anniversary by creating a new ACTRON comic series. Or rather, a new ACTRON comic book. It took the better part of two years to finish this less-than-twenty-page story (with ample assistance from my pal, colorist, and cartoonist in his own right, Pete Toms). Piro and Actron picked up their running dialogue as if no interruption had occurred, and they haven't paused for breath since. I've continued writing novels, comics, zines, short stories, and skits featuring these same obnoxious characters from my youth for something close to an additional fifteen years. You may have noticed the pattern.

It's now late 2020, and I'm beyond tired of listening to this shit. No memory of why I even started up again.

And you know what?

I quit.

SL

remember

massivefictions.com

about the author

Stanley Lieber doesn't want to know.

notes

notes

notes

notes

notes

notes

notes

notes

notes

notes

notes

notes

notes

notes

www.ingramcontent.com/pod-product-compliance
Lightning Source LLC
Chambersburg PA
CBHW030631220526
45463CB00004B/1479